Foreword by

H ow many times have I wondered—have you wondered—what *will* heaven be like? In 1 Corinthians
2:9 (KJV), the apostle Paul wrote, "Eye hath not seen,
nor ear heard, neither have entered into the heart of
man, the things which God hath prepared for them that
love him." Paul knew firsthand of what he wrote since
he had the experience of going to heaven: "I was caught
up to paradise and heard things so astounding that
they cannot be expressed in words, things no human is
allowed to tell" (2 Corinthians 12:4 NLT).

These scriptures, along with the many other refer-
ences to heaven in the Bible—over 600 in the King James
Version alone—stir the hearts of all who look forward to
spending eternity with Jesus. Yet, in the meantime, can
we really know about its streets of gold, the River of Life,
trees that bear twelve kinds of fruit, and the answers to
countless other questions? Most importantly, how do we
get to heaven? What does Scriptures tell us? Well, guess

what—you are in for an adventure as Dr. Billy Graham in *The Heaven Answer Book* takes us by the hand on a glorious Bible tour of our final home!

In this powerful book, Dr. Graham answers the questions we all want to know: What will our new glorified bodies be like? What will we be doing in heaven? What happens when we die? Over 60 questions and answers are provided that will give a better understanding of the glories that await us in that great city where "the Lamb is the light" (Revelation 21:23 KJV).

—Paul F. Crouch, Sr.
President
Trinity Broadcasting Family
of Networks

Presented to:

_____

From:

_____

The
Heaven
ANSWER BOOK

BILLY GRAHAM

THOMAS NELSON
Since 1798

NASHVILLE   DALLAS   MEXICO CITY   RIO DE JANEIRO

Contents

Preface

One of the Bible's greatest truths is that we were not meant for this world alone. We were meant for Heaven—and Heaven is our ultimate home.

But what exactly is Heaven? What is it like, and what (if anything) will we be doing there? Is Heaven something that only affects our future, or should Heaven make a difference in the way we live right now? Most importantly, how can we know we will go there when we die?

These are questions every thoughtful person asks—and God has revealed the answers to them in His Word, the Bible. My purpose in this little volume is to explore those answers, so that we may have hope for the future and meaning for our lives right now.

To accomplish this goal my longtime publisher Thomas Nelson has brought together material on this topic from my writings over the years, and I am grateful to them for compiling and editing it. In addition, I also want to express my thanks to Donna Lee Toney, who compiled and adapted additional material from my writings for this project. May God use it to encourage you to look beyond the burdens and problems of this present world, and to rejoice in the hope we have of Heaven because of Christ's death and resurrection for us.

— Billy Graham

Does Heaven Really Exist?

Praise be to the God and Father of our Lord Jesus Christ! In his great mercy he has given us new birth into a living hope through the resurrection of Jesus Christ from the dead, and into an inheritance that can never perish, spoil or fade—kept in heaven for you.

—1 Peter 1:3–4

Does the Bible say
very much about Heaven?

———————— ✦ ————————

Jesus mentions Heaven about seventy times in the book of Matthew alone. It appears from the very first verse in Genesis—"In the beginning God created the heavens and the earth"—to the last reference found at the end of Revelation—"[He] showed me the great city . . . descending out of heaven from God" (Revelation 21:10 NKJV). In fact, fifty-four of the sixty-six books in the Bible mention Heaven. Remember: the Bible is our only authoritative source of information about Heaven.

Shortly before Jesus was arrested and crucified on the cross, He told His disciples that after His death they should not be discouraged because He would live again. He then assured them He would return to His Father in Heaven to prepare an eternal home for all who would believe Him. He said, "In my Father's house are many rooms; if it were not so, I would have told you." Then He left this promise: "I am going there [to heaven] to prepare a place for you . . . that you also may be where I am" (John 14:2–3).

The Old Testament prophets wrote about Heaven; Psalms mentions Heaven more than any other book in the Old Testament; the apostles spoke of Heaven from divine inspiration from the Holy Spirit. The Bible doesn't tell us everything we'd *like* to know about Heaven, but the Bible does tell us everything we *need* to know about Heaven while we are here on earth. We should believe what the Bible says about Heaven and take comfort from its promise that we can spend eternity with Jesus Christ in His heavenly dwelling.

If someone asks you about Heaven, you can say with assurance, "We know that if the earthly tent [body] we live in is destroyed, we have a building from God, an eternal house in heaven, not built by human hands" (2 Corinthians 5:1). What a promise! What a destiny!

What is Heaven?

Heaven is the place where God dwells—it is God's holy habitation. He created it, He lives there, and, some day, so shall all believers.

Moses prayed that God would "look down from heaven, your holy dwelling place" (Deuteronomy 26:15). Solomon, the wisest king to ever live, prayed: "O LORD my God . . . hear from heaven, your dwelling place" (1 Kings 8:28, 30). Abram said, "God Most High, Creator of heaven" (Genesis 14:22). Nehemiah prayed to "the God of heaven" (Nehemiah 2:4); King Nebuchadnezzar praised the King of Heaven (Daniel 4:37); and Jesus opened our hearts to the reality of Heaven when He lifted His eyes and prayed, "Our Father which art in heaven" (Matthew 6:9 KJV). Heaven is occupied by the presence of Almighty God. This makes Heaven the supreme destination for those who long to worship Him as their Creator, God, Lord, King, Father, and Savior.

This is admittedly hard for us to comprehend; after all, the Bible tells us God is a spirit and is infinite, so how can He be confined to one place? In spite of this mystery, the Bible assures us that His presence fills all of Heaven, and in Heaven we will be safely in His care forever.

The apostle Paul wrote, "Now we see but a poor reflection as in a mirror; then we shall see face to face. Now I know in part; then I shall know fully, even as I am fully known" (1 Corinthians 13:12).

Heaven *is* the Father's house (John 14:2). Heaven *is* the dwelling place of Jesus Christ His Son (1 Peter 3:21–22). Heaven *is* the city of the living God and the redeemed (Hebrews 12:22–23). If this does not fill your heart with hope and a desire for that better country, I urge you to examine where you stand before God, and turn from doubt to belief. If you love Jesus Christ, you will want to follow Him all the way to that place called Heaven. "Many live as enemies of the cross of Christ. Their destiny is destruction. . . . Their mind is on earthly things. But our citizenship is in heaven. And we eagerly await a Savior from there, the Lord Jesus Christ" (Philippians 3:18–20). Paul urges others to follow Him.

Listen with your ears to the voice of God (Ecclesiastes 5:1). *Answer* Christ's knock on your heart's door (Revelation 3:20). *Enter* into fellowship with the Lord Jesus (1 Corinthians 1:9).

This is Heaven.

What do you say to someone who doesn't believe in Heaven?

———————— ✸ ————————

T ell them about Jesus Christ and the hope we have because of His death on the cross for our sins. God sent His Son who gave everything—His very life's blood—His last breath—and His lasting promise—to purchase the souls of men, women, and children for the kingdom of Heaven. Then Jesus rose from the dead by the power of God to confirm Heaven's reality. Believing in Christ settles the question about Heaven!

Recently a young man wrote me, "As far as I'm concerned, once you're dead, that's it. The only life we'll ever experience is the one we're living right now. Life after death is just a myth."

I replied that his letter deeply saddened me, because it meant that he was living without hope: "Have you honestly faced how empty and meaningless this will make your life?" I wrote. "Right now this may not bother you because you're young, healthy, and energetic. But what if something goes wrong? What if you have a serious accident or you lose your health, or someone you love abandons you? Or what will happen once old age creeps up on you with all of its problems and disabilities? You'll be facing the future without any hope. What a terrible thought!" Then I urged him to look at Jesus Christ as He is found in the pages of the New Testament and give his life to Him.

The greatest discovery we will ever make is to know the love of God, which was fully demonstrated by His Son's sacrifice on the cross for us. This is the power that transforms man's myth into Christ's truth. Jesus did not die on the cross for people's sin so that we would believe in Heaven—but that we would believe *in Him*. Heaven does not save souls . . . it collects them.

Jesus once told this parable: "The kingdom of heaven is like a merchant looking for fine pearls. When he found one of great value, he went away and sold everything he had and bought it" (Matthew 13:45–46). The Merchant of Heaven is looking for souls who will love

Him and give Him the worship, glory, and honor due Him. Jesus said, "If anyone loves me, he will obey my teaching. My Father will love him, and we will . . . make our home with him" (John 14:23).

If your hope and faith are not in Christ, then consider what He did for you through His death and resurrection and place your faith in Him today.

Why do most people believe in some kind of life after death, even if they aren't particularly religious or don't think about it very much?

---　✿　---

G od has put within each of us an inner sense that life on earth is not all there is. The Bible answers this so clearly: "[God] has also set eternity in the hearts of men" (Ecclesiastes 3:11).

People may suppress this truth or deny it, but our conscience still speaks. The "still small voice" of God tells us—down deep—that it is still true (1 Kings 19:12). We must never ignore that inner voice—but rather, check what we believe it is saying alongside Scripture, where He reveals these truths.

The apostle Paul wrote about this danger of denying God's truth: "What may be known about God is plain to them, because God has made it plain to them.

For since the creation of the world God's invisible qualities—his eternal power and divine nature—have been clearly seen . . . so that men are without excuse" (Romans 1:19–20).

The reason we have this inner conviction that death is not the end—and that Heaven exists—is because we were created in the image of God. We aren't simply physical beings; we also have a soul (or spirit), and we bear within us the likeness of our Creator. That likeness has been marred and distorted by sin—but it is still there. And just as God is eternal, so we sense in our hearts that we too must be eternal. The Bible says that God lives forever (Isaiah 57:15). Just as God lives forever, we who are made in His likeness will also live forever.

"There is a time for everything . . . under heaven . . . a time to search and a time to give up" (Ecclesiastes 3:1, 6). My prayer is that you will exercise your God-given right to search the Scripture and to seek the One who died for you. Don't give up on God. Instead, give up running *from* God—He hasn't given up on you.

How do we know there is life after death?

———— ✽ ————

We know there is life after death because God promised it, our souls bear witness to it, and most of all, Jesus Christ confirmed it by His life, death, and resurrection. So just look at Jesus. By His resurrection, the Bible says, Jesus Christ "destroyed death and has brought life and immortality to light through the gospel" (2 Timothy 1:10).

Every phase of Jesus' life was miraculous. He set aside His deity, came down to earth, and put on the garment of human suffering. He healed the sick, raised the dead, fed the hungry, quenched the thirsty, and comforted the dispirited with hope for tomorrow. In His compassion for us, He gave up His life to save wandering souls in a confused and dying world. Then He rose again and rejoiced to walk among us as the resurrected Savior, guaranteeing eternal life to all who follow Him.

Look at Jesus. He lived in Heaven and on earth. He died on earth and returned to life *again*, which was witnessed by more than five hundred people (see 1 Corinthians 15:3–8) before returning to Heaven. He lives in the hearts of those who trust in Him. Our confidence in life after death comes from these very truths.

Someone who visited the Billy Graham Library noticed all the crosses displayed and said to her host, "Where is Jesus? Why isn't He on the cross?" Her host smiled and said, "We do not worship a crucifix. Jesus died on the cross, but He did not stay on the cross. . . . He lives!"

The reason life does not end with the grave is because eternity is ahead of us. God's Son conquered death and lives to bring newness of life to all who call on His name (Romans 10:9). This is the hope of the ages!

Listen to the words of the highest authority: "I, Jesus, have sent my angel to give you this testimony . . . 'Come!' . . . Whoever is thirsty, let him come; and whoever wishes, let him take the free gift of the water of life" (Revelation 22:16–17). Gaze at the empty cross and you will see the victorious life over death in Jesus Christ, for in Him "death has been swallowed up in victory" (1 Corinthians 15:54). If you do not know Him, will you call on Him today?

What does the resurrection of Jesus have to do with Heaven?

———————— ✦ ————————

Believing in Heaven has no value if we don't believe in the resurrection of the One who created Heaven and opened its gates to all who will enter. Many people find it easier to believe in Heaven because they've heard about someone's alleged vision, yet they'll doubt that Jesus Christ was raised from the dead and lives in Heaven today. God's Word is our true guide, for it alone points us to the resurrection of Jesus Christ from the dead. Jesus said to Nicodemus, "I have spoken to you of earthly things and you do not believe; how then will you believe if I speak of heavenly things? No one has ever gone into heaven except the one who came from heaven—the Son of Man" (John 3:12–13).

Why is Jesus' resurrection so important? Not only does it prove He was the Son of God and that there is life after death, but it assures us that death—our final enemy—has been defeated. The Bible summarizes this great truth in these words: "For the wages of sin is death, but the gift of God is eternal life in Christ Jesus our Lord" (Romans 6:23).

A remarkable illustration in Scripture is the resurrection of Jesus' friend Lazarus which took place in Bethany where Jesus was also anointed before His death. The Lord gives evidence of His power over the grave of others—and His own grave as well. After Lazarus had been in the grave four days, Jesus demonstrated His resurrection power by raising Lazarus from the dead. When He arrived at the tomb, He called with a loud voice: "Lazarus, come forth!" and Lazarus emerged from the grave and stood before the crowd (John 11:43 NKJV). This proved Jesus' power over death—and also the truth of His promise to us: "I am the resurrection and the life. He who believes in me will live, even though he dies; and whoever lives and believes in me will never die. Do you believe this?" (vv. 25–26).

Heaven comes to life for us because of Christ's

resurrection power. If you will sincerely search for Him, you will find new life in Christ. The resurrection is the fulfillment of the Word of God, and that fact authenticates Heaven!

Does God allow some people to have a glimpse of Heaven just before they die or even earlier? Did it happen to anyone in the Bible?

While Scripture does not promise a glimpse into Heaven, it does tell of an account of Stephen, the first person to be martyred for his faith in Christ, who declared as he was being stoned, "I see heaven open and the Son of Man standing at the right hand of God" (Acts 7:56).

Some claim to have died and gone to Heaven and returned to tell what they saw and experienced. Others tell about visiting Heaven, but Heaven is not a retreat or a place to visit—it is a permanent dwelling. Claims about eyewitness accounts of Heaven often say little about Jesus Christ—and this should make us treat them with great caution. Our hope must be built on

Christ alone and on the promises God has given us in His Word.

Death is the universal fate of every human being. It is the end of life on earth—but the beginning of eternal life in Heaven with God or everlasting torment in that place apart from God, Hell. I have talked to doctors and nurses who have held the hands of the dying, and they say there is often as much difference between the death of a Christian and a non-Christian as there is between Heaven and Hell. Glimpsing Heaven would be a grand vision for those who are certain it is their destination. For those who have never settled eternity in their hearts, Heaven is elusive.

It's important to respond to Christ while we are still living. Have you responded to His call? Jesus' invitation is for you: "Come to me, all you who are weary and burdened, and I will give you rest" (Matthew 11:28).

Is Heaven a literal place, simply a state of mind, or kind of a dream?

―――――― ✦ ――――――

Heaven is a literal place. It is not an imaginary world or fantasy land in which to dwell.

God created Heaven with its vast array of authentic characteristics (Genesis 2:1). Jesus did not ascend to a lofty dreamworld following His resurrection, but returned to sit at the right hand of God (Mark 16:19). Abraham didn't cling to the promise of living in a state of mind; he looked forward to "the city with foundations, whose architect and builder is God" (Hebrews 11:10). The Old Testament heroes of faith longed for a literal place—"a better country—a heavenly one . . . for [God] has prepared a city for them" (v. 16). Jesus told His disciples, "You know the way to the place where I am going" (John 14:4). That place is Heaven and Christ our Savior is there now, preparing for our arrival.

Having confidence that Heaven is a literal place is

important, but even more so is that we know how to get there. The only GPS that can give you flawless direction is the Gospel Plan of Salvation. Jesus said, "I am the way and the truth and the life. No one comes to the Father except through me" (John 14:6).

By nature, people are bent toward home. Far better than any dream you can imagine is the supernatural transformation that will take place for all of God's people in His heavenly home. I hope you'll be there.

Where is Heaven? Is it off in space somewhere?

❋

The Bible tells us that God set a firmament in the midst of the waters, divided the waters from the waters, and called the firmament "Heaven" (Genesis 1:6–8 NKJV). The word *firmament* is one we aren't accustomed to hearing anymore; it comes from a Hebrew word meaning "firm" or "fixed." The Bible clearly defines Heaven as a created place. God said, "My own hand laid the foundations of the earth, and my right hand spread out the heavens" (Isaiah 48:13; 1 Corinthians 2:9).

While Heaven captures our imagination, it's more important that the God of Heaven captures our souls; for God is greater than Heaven. The Bible says, "The heavens . . . cannot contain [Him]" (1 Kings 8:27)—but He can contain His whole creation in His hands. He measured the waters in the hollow of His hand, marked off the Heavens, held the dust of the earth in a basket, and weighed the mountains on scales (Isaiah 40:12).

The Bible says, "No eye has seen, no ear has heard, no mind has conceived what God has prepared for those who love him" (1 Corinthians 2:9).

Just because Heaven is beyond the reach of man's satellites and telescopes, however, does not mean that Heaven is beyond the reach of our hearts. The Bible says, "[Christ] is the image of the invisible God . . . by him all things were created: things in heaven and on earth, visible and invisible . . . all things were created by him and for him" (Colossians 1:15–16). Heaven is where the Lord is, and Christ is Lord of Heaven and earth. He is able to rule from Heaven and also live within our hearts.

Will earth be an extension of Heaven some day?

———— ✦ ————

Yes, the Bible tells us that God will bring Heaven to earth where He will live among His people at the end of this present age.

In that day, the old will be destroyed, a new earth will be created, and there will truly be Heaven on earth. The apostle Peter wrote, "We are looking forward to a new heaven and a new earth, the home of righteousness" (2 Peter 3:13).

When God created the world, the first book in the Old Testament tells us He spoke Heaven and earth and the seas into existence (Genesis 1:6–9). In the last book of the New Testament, Christ tells John to write down His revelation of the future. "Then I saw a new heaven and a new earth, for the first heaven and the first earth had passed away, and there was no longer any sea. I saw the Holy City . . . coming down out of heaven from God. . . . And I heard a loud voice from the throne saying, 'Now the dwelling of God is with men, and he will live with them.' . . . He who was seated on the throne said, 'I am making everything new!'" (Revelation 21:1–3, 5).

Earth cannot promise anything eternal. Earth's value will plummet when Heaven comes down with the glory of God. Someday the earth as we know it will pass away, but God's Word will never pass away—and that is why we can say with assurance that earth has no hold on us. The Old Testament saints declared themselves strangers and aliens on earth, and we, too, should hold loosely the things of this world because they will not last. When Heaven comes down, earthly things will fall away and the goodness of God will reign.

What Is Heaven Like?

And I heard a loud voice from the throne saying, "Now the dwelling of God is with men, and he will live with them. They will be his people, and God himself will be with them and be their God. He will wipe every tear from their eyes. There will be no more death or mourning or crying or pain, for the old order of things has passed away."

—Revelation 21:3–4

What is the main difference between earth and Heaven?

———— ✸ ————

The main difference between earth and Heaven is that this world has been corrupted by sin—but Heaven has not. Man's sin permeates the earth, and God's glory perfects Heaven.

God, the glory of Heaven, created earth and gave it to the human race to care for and enjoy. Instead of obeying God's instruction concerning the things of earth, however, Adam and Eve chose to listen to Satan and do the only thing God had forbidden them to do. Their disobedience—their rebellion against God—cursed the earth, and separated them from fellowship with God. "For as by one man's disobedience many were made sinners" (Romans 5:19 NKJV). As a result, the disease of sin has been passed to every generation. The Bible says, "God saw how corrupt the earth had become, for all the people on earth had corrupted their ways" (Genesis 6:12). "Earth is defiled by its people. . . . Therefore a curse consumes the earth; its people must bear their guilt" (Isaiah 24:5–6).

The earth groans because it has been marred by sin; like a crippling disease, sin distorts and devastates everything it touches. Sin corrupts and divides, but Heaven declares the glory of the Lord (Psalm 19:1). Heaven is the throne of God (Isaiah 66:1), and because He is absolutely holy and without sin, He cannot tolerate sin or look upon it without bringing judgment. The Bible says of God, "Your eyes are too pure to look on evil; you cannot tolerate wrong" (Habakkuk 1:13).

But His love is so powerful and great that He made a way for sin's curse to be removed—the guilt that stains our hearts and corrupts our world. God crucified sin on the cross by the blood of Christ who redeemed us from sin's penalty. He died in our place, taking the judgment we deserve, presenting us faultless to His Father in Heaven. Jesus Christ is the Savior of the world because He is the only One who can bridge the gap *between* Heaven and earth. The Bible says, "By one Man's obedience many will be made righteous" (Romans 5:19 NKJV).

It's hard for us to admit, but we are sinners by birth, sinners by choice, and sinners by practice. The good news is that God has made a way for us to be saved by His grace (Ephesians 2:8–9), and this is His glorious gift to people in a fallen world. The difference between Heaven and earth is that Jesus Christ left Heaven's glory and came to this sin-infested earth for one reason: to make our eternal salvation possible. And that makes all the difference—to God in Heaven and to us on earth.

What will we see when we get to Heaven?

────────── ❋ ──────────

We will see many glorious sites in Heaven, but the most wonderful of all will be the Savior of the world and His glory. "Your eyes will see the king in his beauty and view a land that stretches afar" (Isaiah 33:17).

Jesus Christ gave us a glimpse of this when He pulled back the curtain of Heaven and told the apostle John to write down what he saw: "Then I saw a Lamb . . . I heard every creature in heaven . . . singing: 'To him who sits on the throne and to the Lamb be praise and honor and glory and power for ever and ever!'" (Revelation 5:6, 13).

It is part of our human nature to want to satisfy our imaginations about Heaven, but God has His reasons for giving us only a taste of His eternal dwelling. Human language falls short of describing such majesty. The magnificence of earth's possessions will dim in Heaven's sunlight. John could only express it with analogies: "Its brilliance was like that of a very precious jewel, like jasper, clear as crystal. . . . The great street of the city was of pure gold, like transparent glass" (Revelation 21:11, 21). Here on earth, streets are covered with gravel and asphalt, and windows are made of glass, but John writes about the golden streets that are transparent. Keep in mind that in Heaven everything is made new. We are given only snapshots of things to come. We will require a heavenly transformation to comprehend such glory.

Clouded things of earth will become transparent in eternity; now they are known only by Him. As we practice patience while waiting, let thoughts of Heaven's glory fill your soul. They will sustain you until the day your eyes are fully opened.

Peter tells those whose hope is heavenward, "You will receive a rich welcome into the eternal kingdom of our Lord and Savior Jesus Christ" (2 Peter 1:11). When He extends His arms inviting His people in, He will turn to His Father and say, "I have given them the glory that you gave me, that they may be one as we are one" (John 17:22). We will gaze at His nail-scarred hands, fall at His feet, and weep with joy, praising His wonderful name. That's what we'll see in Heaven.

Is anything about Heaven imperfect or incomplete?

―――――― ⊛ ――――――

Heaven isn't only glorious—it is also perfect. You see, sin has no home in Heaven. The Bible says, "Nothing impure will ever enter it, nor will anyone who does what is shameful or deceitful" (Revelation 21:27). Human minds cannot conceive such purity because we are a race of fallen creatures plagued with disease, consumed with war, enraged by jealousy, dejected by loneliness, jaded by greed, enticed by temptation, disappointed by others, conflicted within, and demonized by Satan. This describes what the writer of Hebrews said, "Let us throw off everything that hinders and the sin that so easily entangles" (12:1). Those who know and follow Jesus as Lord recognize sin's evil results.

If you've ever traveled through a construction zone, you know it can be perilous. Travelers are relieved when they see a sign posted that says "End of Construction" and they no longer have to watch for the caution flags or dodge the cones in the way. This is a picture of the Christian life, and we must stay alert as we journey through it. The "potholes" we encounter on this journey jolt us, and the "detours" get us off track, but the Lord uses them to guide and strengthen our faith.

Before my wife, Ruth, died in 2007, she asked that the words "End of Construction: Thank You for Your Patience" be engraved on her grave marker. It brings a smile to everyone who visits her resting place. She recognized an important message in those words. When we reach the end of the journey, our construction is complete on earth and transformation awaits us in Heaven. As the Bible says, "He who began a good work in you will carry it on to completion until the day of Christ Jesus" (Philippians 1:6).

The apostle James said, "Perseverance must finish its work so that you may be mature and complete, not lacking anything" (James 1:4). We will lack nothing in Heaven. God is patient, knowing that we are imperfect people—but we have a perfect Savior. What a wonderful promise from God's Word to those of us on earth: "Dear friends, now we are children of God, and what we will be has not yet been made known. But we know that when he appears, we shall be like him, for we shall see him as he is" (1 John 3:2). Once in His presence, we will finally be complete because we will be transformed into His likeness.

Can we be assured that Heaven can make us perfect?

————————— ✵ —————————

I n Heaven we will be perfect—but by itself, Heaven cannot perfect anything or anyone; Heaven cannot save us. Only God—the Master Resident and Kingdom Title-Owner, who makes Heaven and all of its residents perfect—can do this. So while Heaven reflects the perfection of its Ruler, it is the Lord Himself who perfects His saints.

The Bible has much to say about the perfection of the One who occupies Heaven's glory. "Listen, O heavens, and I will speak. . . . He is the Rock, his works are perfect, and all his ways are just. A faithful God who does no wrong, upright and just is he" (Deuteronomy 32:1, 4). The heavens declare that God's instruction is perfect (Psalm 19:1, 7). His peace is perfect (Isaiah 26:3); God's will is perfect (Romans 12:2); the Father in Heaven is perfect (Matthew 5:48); Jesus Christ is the perfect leader

(Hebrews 2:10); and He alone is the perfect sacrifice (Hebrews 9:11).

Only the One who *is* perfection can perfect others: "By one sacrifice he has made perfect forever those who are being made holy" (Hebrews 10:14).

You may ask how we can be assured of this. Because the Bible says so—it is *the* reason. God's Word is the ultimate authority that needs no other supporting documentation or testimony. The Scripture says, "'The Lord has sworn and will not change his mind . . .' Because of this oath, Jesus has become the guarantee of a better covenant. Therefore he is able to save completely those who come to God through him" (Hebrews 7:21–22, 25).

Take a moment to consider what it means for Christ to *save completely*. We like to think about the prospects of Heaven's joy—but what *won't* we miss in Heaven? When we are cloaked in Christ's perfection, there will be no more sin, no more physical pain, no more mental anguish, no more loneliness, no more daily stress, no more abuse, no more weariness or lack of strength, no more aging process, no more death. Nothing from Satan will ever enter our glorified state. We can't fathom what God has in store for us when He makes all creation new. Believe it by faith and share with those who still doubt that they, too, can be perfected in Heaven by turning to Christ and abandoning their unobtainable satisfaction on earth.

Will Heaven be somber and serious?

———— ✱ ————

The Bible says that *joy* will be the heavenly mood (Romans 14:17). This is a theme referenced in Scripture nearly two hundred times!

I can remember returning home from Bible school for the holidays, filled with anticipation. Mother had baked some of my favorite dishes and my father listened patiently to all I was learning. I wanted to show my respect and honor by taking seriously the investment they were making in my future and our home was filled with joy.

This is but a glimpse of the relationship we will have with the Lord in Heaven. Our emotions and thoughts will be perfectly expressed before the throne of God. The Bible says the Kingdom of God is a place of "righteousness, peace, and joy in the Holy Spirit" (Romans 14:17).

The Lord said, "My own hands stretched out the heavens; I marshaled their starry hosts" (Isaiah 45:12).

In the heavenly ages to come, we will better comprehend the starry hosts He calls by name. We will cast our eyes on His hands that bear the marks of why we will be permitted through Heaven's gates instead of standing accused before God's throne—because Christ will have presented us faultless, with exceeding joy (Jude 24). The ransomed of the Lord will be overtaken with joy, and "sorrow and sighing will flee away" (Isaiah 51:11). The psalmist declared, "You will fill me with joy in your presence" (Psalm 16:11).

Yes, we will take seriously all that God has done for us. And we will take pleasure in His attributes, for the fruit of His Spirit is joy (Galatians 5:22).

When Jesus was on earth, He said that He would give us His joy (John 15:11) and that it would be complete and never be taken away (John 16:22). And the Lord keeps His promises. He would not give us something so wonderful as His joy on earth and then take it away in Heaven. Among the many promises of God, He said, "My people will receive a double portion . . . and everlasting joy will be theirs" (Isaiah 61:7).

Will we recognize and be reunited with our loved ones?

———————— ✦ ————————

I am often asked this question—and my answer is always a resounding yes. Someday soon, I know I will be reunited with all those in my family who are already in Heaven—including my wife, Ruth.

And when it happens for each believer, we will fellowship around our Father's throne, finally meeting Him face-to-face. And the family of God—our brothers and sisters in Christ—will be there. This is why it's so important for us to tell our loved ones about Christ. Nothing is more wonderful than for our families to share in this great hope of being part of the heavenly family.

Jesus in His resurrected body was known to His followers. When Christ was transfigured and His heavenly glory overwhelmed His earthly appearance, Moses and Elijah appeared with Him before Peter, James, and John (Matthew 17:1–3). Though the disciples had never seen the great prophets, they recognized them, just as they recognized the Lord in His transfigured state. These examples give us great hope that we will know those we knew on earth and even others we've never met.

Often the question is asked if those who die as infants will be in Heaven. I have no doubt that they will be. God is the God of hope and salvation, and we can say as King David said when his infant son died, "Can I bring him back again? I will go to him" (2 Samuel 12:23).

Jesus Himself said, "Many will come from the east and the west, and will take their places at the feast with Abraham, Isaac and Jacob in the kingdom of heaven" (Matthew 8:11). I long to meet not only my loved ones in Heaven, but also the prophets and the apostles and the mother of our Lord. But my greatest expectation is to gaze into the eyes of Jesus, who knows me by name.

The writer of Hebrews wrote: "But we see Jesus . . . bringing many sons to glory. . . . Both the one who makes men holy and those who are made holy are of the same family. So Jesus is not ashamed to call them brothers. He says, 'I will declare your name to my brothers. . . . Here am I, and the children God has given me'" (2:9–13).

What a marvelous reunion when the family of God gathers in Heaven to praise His name!

Will our worship in Heaven be like our worship on earth?

———— ✹ ————

Worship on earth cannot compare to the perfected worship of the saints in Heaven. It won't be about us—it will be about Him. Jesus said, "A time is coming . . . when the true worshipers will worship the Father . . . for they are the kind of worshipers the Father seeks. . . . His worshipers must worship in spirit and in truth" (John 4:23–24). He was responding to the Samaritan woman at the well, who was focused only on the *place* of worship rather than the *Person* she should worship. Jesus knew that the day would come when places of worship would be destroyed. He was moving her heart from the place of worship to the Person to be worshiped.

We are living in perilous times, watching the name of Christ attacked both from outside the church and also from within. At times Satan and his demons have disguised themselves as sheep and have slipped in among believers, causing division, confusion, and deception. Jesus said, "Away from me, Satan! For it is written: 'Worship the Lord your God, and serve him only'" (Matthew 4:10). The Bible says, "Certain men . . . have secretly slipped in among you. They are godless men, who change the grace of our God into a license for immorality and deny Jesus Christ our only Sovereign and Lord" (Jude 4). Scripture warns against worshiping created things rather than the Creator (Romans 1:25). This is certainly evident in our society today; in some circles, we are even dangerously close to *worshiping our worship*.

Worship on earth can easily take the form of mindless activity or superficial entertainment. Many have come to believe that worship is only singing songs and clapping our hands. But true worship is focusing on Christ and living for Him day by day, in spirit and in truth. The center of true worship is the Lord.

Even at our best, our worship on earth will always be imperfect, incomplete, and even superficial and boring at times. In Heaven, *our worship* will be transformed.

Our spirits will not feed on satisfying ourselves. *Our minds* will be fixed on Him. *Our hearts* will be filled with thanksgiving. And *our lips* will express the adoration due His name.

Will we have work to do in Heaven or will we just sit around and do nothing?

---⚙---

God never intended for people to be idle and un-productive—on earth or in Heaven. Heaven is about serving—not ourselves, but Jesus Christ: "The throne of God and of the Lamb will be in the city, and his servants will serve him" (Revelation 22:3).

We will have the highest honor of serving God in Heaven, and our joy will be full, because we will reign with Christ forever (Revelation 22:5). The Lord has always been at work—creating, forgiving, loving, comforting, correcting, guiding. And certainly the greatest work Jesus did was not in the carpenter's shop in Nazareth, but rather, during those three dark hours on the cross, dying for us. Still today, Jesus Christ is at work in Heaven, interceding for us. Jesus said, "My Father is always at his work to this very day, and I, too, am working" (John 5:17).

In Heaven, God observed a day of rest after creating the world in six days—but nothing in the Scriptures indicates He took a day of rest because He was tired. When we receive our Heavenly bodies, we will also work and not grow weary. And we will have rest; the Bible says that "they will rest from their labor, for their deeds will follow them" (Revelation 14:13).

God placed Adam in the Garden of Eden in perfect conditions and told him "to work it and take care of it" (Genesis 2:15). When God created the animals, He brought them to Adam to "see what he would name them; and whatever the man called each living creature, that was its name" (Genesis 2:19). If God gave man pleasurable work on earth in the beginning, then the same will be true in Heaven. There will be no drudgery in Heaven.

Heaven is a place of service, and those who are going there long to hear Him say, "Well done, good and faithful servant. . . . Enter into the joy of your lord" (Matthew 25:21 NKJV).

Will we live in literal mansions or palaces in Heaven?

———— ✸ ————

The Bible assures us that in Heaven we will be living in God's dwelling place forever, and it will be glorious beyond description. It will be greater than any earthly palace or mansion.

Kings are confined to living in palaces. Owners of vast properties live on estates behind locked gates. God's Word, however, says that Christ will make us joint heirs in the Kingdom of God—and just as God's habitation extends *beyond* the boundaries of creation, so will ours—without confinement.

He owns it all and is going to share it with His people. He is the King and landowner of Heaven, earth, and the whole universe. No earthly court, no Wall Street investor, no astute accountant could ever calculate the extent of God's estate—for it is priceless.

Jesus told His disciples, "I confer on you a kingdom,

just as my Father conferred one on me" (Luke 22:29). So when Jesus, the heir of this incalculable estate tells us, "I go to prepare a place for you" we cannot fathom what He has in store. But we do know that "the Spirit himself testifies with our spirit that we are God's children. Now if we are children, then we are heirs—heirs of God and co-heirs with Christ" (Romans 8:16–17).

For most of my adult life, I have lived in a comfortable log house on top of a mountain, and I love this place. My wife, Ruth, oversaw the building of our home and though she's no longer here, her touches are in every room. We raised our five children here, and watched them explore every hideaway and clump of trees around our home. These are fond memories. But I'm looking forward to a better home—a perfect home—whose Builder and Maker is God. It will have no flaws, because it is the House of the Lord—and "on no day will its gates ever be shut" (Revelation 21:25). The day I step through the gates of splendor, I'll finally be free of the confinements of earth.

Will there be animals in Heaven?

———————— ✦ ————————

G od's creation story is the first miraculous account in the Bible which includes His creation of animals. While the Bible does not specifically answer this question, no one can miss God's creative work in the animal kingdom. His written Word provides us with a snapshot of His original handiwork: "Let the earth bring forth the living creature according to its kind: cattle . . . and everything . . . on the earth. . . . And God saw that it was good" (Genesis 1:24–25 NKJV). All this took place *before* sin entered the world.

I grew up on a farm, and animals have always fascinated me. We know that God gave them to us for a purpose, because in the days of Noah, before the great Flood, God preserved every species—male and female—on the ark so they would inhabit the land again. Animals are among God's many diverse gifts to man. Who doesn't smile while watching chimpanzees mimic one another?

We boast of "man's best friend" because a faithful dog will protect its owner at all cost. Fish are a source of food, and we love to envision Jesus sharing broiled fish with His disciples (Luke 24:42–43). We marvel to think of Jesus riding the colt of a donkey into Jerusalem—and we wait breathlessly for His appearance on a white horse from Heaven (Revelation 19:11).

Scripture speaks of the future messianic kingdom that captivates our imagination: "The wolf will live with the lamb, the leopard will lie down with the goat, the calf and the lion and the yearling together; and a little child will lead them" (Isaiah 11:6). In that day, death and evil will be destroyed, perfect peace will reign, and everything that has breath, including animals, will praise Him (Psalm 150:6). What a day that will be!

Will there be fear in Heaven?

———————— ✦ ————————

F ear will not be present in God's eternal kingdom. We won't need locks on the doors, or bars on the windows, or alarm systems warning of intruders. Everything that causes us fear right now will be eliminated.

Fear is a powerful emotion with many dimensions, and the one that affects us most is described as "distressing emotion aroused by impending danger, evil, pain—whether real or imagined."

If we were familiar with another of fear's definitions, however, it would cancel out the preceding one. You see, *fear* can also mean "reverential awe"—giving full respect to our holy God, who will execute judgment on the unrighteous. Those who dwell with the Righteous One will have nothing to fear, however. The Bible says, "Fear of man will prove to be a snare, but whoever trusts in the LORD is kept safe" (Proverbs 29:25). This is why the phrase "fear not" runs throughout Scripture. Victory over evil will prevail in the kingdom of God. John writes, "Perfect love drives out fear" (1 John 4:18).

Today, fear stalks the world. Even though the psalmist said, "In God I have put my trust; I will not fear" (Psalm 56:4 NKJV)—in our frail humanness, fear still creeps in. Jesus knew this and said, "Do not be afraid, little flock, for your Father has been pleased to give you the kingdom" (Luke 12:32).

Everything in Heaven is made perfect by God, and His perfect love will conquer all our fears. In Heaven, we are promised unending reverential fellowship with our holy God, who will destroy all evil forever. The Bible says, "In righteousness you will be established. . . . Terror will be far removed; it will not come near you" (Isaiah 54:14).

I have spent my life preaching good news, and here is some good news: In Heaven "there will be no more death or mourning or crying or pain, for the old order of things has passed away" (Revelation 21:4). The heavenly kingdom will be filled with all that is pure. That's good news!

Will there be suffering or
death in Heaven?

---⊛---

No, there will be no suffering and death in Heaven. When something is full, nothing can be added— and the Bible says that Heaven is filled with the glory of the Lord.

Physical death will come to believers in Jesus Christ (except those living at the time of the rapture), but believers are assured that there will be no second death for those who have been redeemed. "He who overcomes will not be hurt at all by the second death" (Revelation 2:11).

The Bible says that Jesus suffered the taste of death for everyone, bringing many people to glory, and making salvation perfect through that suffering which leads to joy (Hebrews 2:9–10; 1 Peter 4:13). Had Christ not conquered death on earth, there would be no eternal life in Heaven. But He did conquer death! The Bible says, "Blessed and holy are those who have part in the first resurrection. The second death has no power over them, but they will . . . reign with him" (Revelation 20:6).

Despair, in any form, will not be permitted to taint our life in Heaven, for God has promised that He will wipe every tear away (Revelation 21:4). The Bible tells us our souls will "be like a well-watered garden" and we will "sorrow no more" (Jeremiah 31:12). The Lord declared, "I fill heaven" (Jeremiah 23:24). There will be no funerals there.

Will there be night or darkness in Heaven?

━━━━━━━ ❋ ━━━━━━━

There will be no darkness in Heaven. The Bible says, "The city [of God] does not need the sun or the moon to shine on it, for the glory of God gives it light, and the Lamb is its lamp. . . . There will be no night there" (Revelation 21:23, 25).

Darkness is often the backdrop for evil works and secrecy. Scripture says, "Men loved darkness instead of light . . . and will not come into the light for fear that [their] deeds will be exposed" (John 3:19–20). Judas led a mob "carrying torches, lanterns and weapons" to Jesus, betraying our Lord in the darkness of night (John 18:3). As believers, however, "we do not belong to the night or to the darkness" (1 Thessalonians 5:5).

When light shines in the night, however, it can bring a ray of hope. The glory of the Lord shone around the shepherds watching their flocks by night when an angel appeared and declared, "I bring you good news . . . a Savior has been born to you" (Luke 2:10–11). Night could never have a beauty of its own were it not for the glowing stars God has suspended in the sky. When God began His work of creation, the earth was covered with darkness. He said, "'Let there be light,' and there was light. God saw that the light was good" (Genesis 1:3–4).

When I was a boy and dusk settled across the farm, my mother lit the lamps that illuminated our house, because our work was not done and we needed light. The Bible says the day is coming that Jesus will snuff out the dim light of this world, and His people will walk the banks of the River of Life in the light of His glory, having been called out of darkness into His marvelous light (1 Peter 2:9). And in that everlasting light our work— His work—will continue.

Will there be denominations in Heaven?

———————— ✸ ————————

There will be no denominations in Heaven. "The Lord God Almighty and the Lamb are its temple" (Revelation 21:22). Then Jesus' prayer will be fulfilled: "That they may be one as we are one" (John 17:11).

The church—the body of Christ—is far greater than any building or denomination. It is the vast fellowship of men and women throughout the ages who belong to Christ. Paul wrote of "God's household . . . the church of the living God" (1 Timothy 3:15).

Heavenly worship will not take place at Faith Temple or Community Chapel. John tells us about our place of worship in the Holy City: "Behold, the tabernacle of God is with men. . . . I saw no temple in it, for the Lord God Almighty and the Lamb are its temple" (Revelation 21:3, 22 NKJV). The tabernacle of God will be the center of all worship and praise.

People organized denominations; Jesus instituted

the church and called it "my church" (Matthew 16:18), made up of those who belong to Christ. He is the Cornerstone (1 Peter 2:6) and the head of the church (Ephesians 5:23). He calls it a spiritual house, a house of prayer, and His body (1 Corinthians 12:27). Its commission is to "go into all the world and preach the gospel" (Mark 16:15 NKJV).

We will be welcomed into Heaven because of our position in Christ, not because of our church or Sunday school credentials. The Bible says, "You have come . . . to the city of the living God . . . to the general assembly and church of the firstborn who are registered in heaven, to God. . . . See that you do not refuse Him" (Hebrews 12:22–23, 25 NKJV).

Jesus gave the keys of the kingdom of Heaven to the church and sent the Holy Spirit to indwell it (Matthew 16:19). Christ's followers were first called Christians (Acts 11:26) and the church was known as "The Way" (Acts 9:2). No better name describes how to be part of it: "I am the way and the truth and the life. No one comes to the Father except through me" (John 14:6).

Let's be faithful, then, with the work God has given us on earth, so that those we meet every day will have the opportunity to turn to Christ and worship the Savior with us in the tabernacle of God.

Will there be eating and drinking in Heaven?

--- ✻ ---

Jesus assured His disciples that some day they would "eat and drink at my table in my kingdom" (Luke 22:30).

Some have speculated that glorified bodies will not require food for sustenance, but the Lord promised, "I will give the right to eat from the tree of life, which is in the paradise of God" (Revelation 2:7). And John gives us a glimpse of this revelation: "On each side of the river stood the tree of life, bearing twelve crops of fruit, yielding its fruit every month" (Revelation 22:2). This would indicate a bountiful supply from Creator God.

Remember too that when Jesus appeared to His followers in His glorified body, He asked them if there were anything to eat. Luke reports that "they gave him a piece of broiled fish . . . and [He] ate it in their presence" (Luke 24:42–43). It wasn't that Jesus was hungry, for He was no longer subject to human needs. I believe He ate with them for two reasons: to prove His bodily resurrection and for fellowship with His disciples. When He was last with them, they fellowshipped around the table and shared the Passover meal.

After all, what would a family reunion be without food? When the family of God assembles in His kingdom, we will enjoy Heaven-blessed food with the Lamb! He will look into the souls gathered around the Lord's Table, and His heart will be full. "People will come . . . and will take their places at the feast in the kingdom of God" (Luke 13:29).

Before that day, however, don't overlook every opportunity God gives you to "taste and see that the LORD is good" (Psalm 34:8).

What Happens
When We Die?

Even though I walk
    through the valley of the shadow of death,
I will fear no evil,
    for you are with me;
your rod and your staff,
    they comfort me. . . .
Surely goodness and love will follow me
    all the days of my life,
and I will dwell in the house of the LORD
    forever.

—Psalm 23:4, 6

Why must we die?

———————— ✹ ————————

Death is the penalty for sin—and because we are all infected with the disease of sin, we are all subject to death. The Bible says, "For the wages of sin is death" (Romans 6:23).

Death was never part of God's original plan. God told Adam and Eve, "You are free to eat from any tree in the garden; but you must not eat from the tree of the knowledge of good and evil, for when you eat of it you will surely die" (Genesis 2:16–17).

There was nothing magical about the tree, but God had every right to withhold it from Adam and Eve and shield them from the knowledge of evil. But Satan was determined to make what was *forbidden* look attractive to Adam and Eve. The sin they committed was disobedience to God . . . and in time, they died—as God had warned. Satan's lie that they would "be like God" overpowered them and made them forget all the provisions

God had graciously given them (Genesis 3:5–7). This is the sin that saturates our hearts to this day—to believe Satan's deceitful lies instead of respecting and honoring God's gracious gifts.

Death is the common lot of every living thing: people, plants, and animals. Death afflicts all creation. From the moment a child is born, the dying process—and the fight against it—begins. But God, in His great love, made it possible for us to have victory over death, in spite of the fact that we must walk through it. The Bible tells us that death cannot separate believers in Jesus Christ from the love of God (Romans 8:38–39). The Bible also says, "I have set before you life and death, blessings and curses. Now choose life, so that you and your children may live. . . . For the LORD is your life" (Deuteronomy 30:19–20).

The death of the righteous is not to be feared or shunned. It is the shadowed threshold to Heaven—the palace of God.

Why are we afraid to die?

————————— ❁ —————————

We are afraid to die because we cannot see beyond this present world. Death reduces all of us to the same rank. It strips the rich of their millions and the poor of their rags. Death knows no age limits, no partiality. It is that which all men fear.

For some, it is the process of dying that is so frightful; even the most devout are susceptible to this fear. King David said, "Terrors of death assail me" (Psalm 55:4). The disciples cried out to the Lord, "Save us! We're going to drown!" (Matthew 8:25).

For others it is the uncertainty of what happens *after* they die, so that death carries with it a sense of dread. It is the enemy—the great, mysterious monster that makes people quake with fear. Yet when it came time for David to die, he expressed assurance of the afterlife and "spoke of the resurrection of the Christ, that he was not abandoned to the grave, nor did his body see decay" (Acts 2:31). The disciples, who had once feared death on the Sea of Galilee, crisscrossed the world proclaiming that death had been swallowed up in victory because of Christ's resurrection.

Why live in a sea of despair when you can live knowing that, after death, life can be experienced as it was originally intended—in fellowship with our Creator and our Lord? This is the confidence that Christians possess. Death marks the beginning of a new and wonderful life in Heaven with Christ that will last forever. To the believer, death is merely the gateway to eternal life, where "underneath are the everlasting arms" (Deuteronomy 33:27).

How do we know our souls won't be trapped in our bodies when we die?

———— ✦ ————

There's one very good reason: God has promised to take us to Himself when we die. The Bible says, "We know that if the earthly tent we live in [our body] is destroyed, we have a building from God, an eternal house in heaven" (2 Corinthians 5:1).

Jesus said our souls, which are His very creation, are more valuable to Him than all the rest of the world put together. The Bible teaches us that our bodies are flesh and bone, and they will die eventually—but that we also are immortal, eternal souls. The soul (or spirit) includes our conscience, as well as the part of us that thinks, feels, and dreams. It will never die, but will live forever in either Heaven or Hell. Most of all, through our souls we can know God and have fellowship with Him.

When God created Adam, He formed his body from the dust of the ground. That body was not living until

God breathed into it "the breath of life, and the man became a living being" (Genesis 2:7). When a person dies, the body gives up the ravages of age and disease to decay, but the spirit (soul) returns to its Maker: "Dust returns to the ground it came from, and the spirit returns to God who gave it" (Ecclesiastes 12:7). Paul declared that to be in Heaven is "to be away from the body and at home with the Lord" (2 Corinthians 5:8).

Have you ever wanted to go somewhere, but you were just too tired? Your body stays home, but your thoughts are where you wish you could be. This is a picture of the separation of body and soul. The body will be buried in the earth awaiting the final resurrection, but the soul will be in God's care.

We may spend all of our time pampering our bodies, but if we ignore our souls, we will end up spiritually starved. While we're here, we must take care of our souls—and God's treasure—by feeding on the Word of God, for our soul is the only thing we can take out of our earthly experience to Heaven.

Are we immediately with the Lord in Heaven when we die, or do we have a time of "soul sleep" before we go into God's presence?

———— ✸ ————

The Bible teaches "to be absent from the body and to be present with the Lord" (2 Corinthians 5:8 NKJV). The apostle Paul, writing in the midst of his struggles in prison, yearned for the glories that awaited him when his body would be killed and he would be in the Lord's presence: "I desire to depart and be with Christ, which is better by far" (Philippians 1:23).

The apostle John had a different experience in prison. When he was given a vision of Heaven, he described the glimpse he had of "the souls of those who had been slain because of the word of God" (Revelation 6:9). These were Christian martyrs, and John heard them crying out and asking when the Lord would avenge their blood.

John heard the Voice say to them, "Rest a little while longer" (v. 6:11 NKJV). Here is a picture of souls at rest in the presence of God. While their bodies are still in the grave awaiting the final resurrection, God's Spirit comforts their spirits because He is the God of all comfort. Jesus said, "[God] is not the God of the dead, but of the living" (Mark 12:27). One of the comforts of being a Christian is the glorious hope that extends beyond the grave into the glory of God's tomorrow. As Jesus declared to the repentant criminal who was crucified with Him, "I tell you the truth, *today* you will be with me in paradise" (Luke 23:43, emphasis added).

Do angels accompany the dead to Heaven?

---✦---

We actually have a glimpse of this in the story Jesus told of the rich man and the beggar named Lazarus. When the beggar died, Jesus said, "the angels carried him to Abraham's side [another term for Heaven]" (Luke 16:22).

Many accounts tell of dying saints being at peace because of this angelic presence. The Lord is the God of all comfort, and He employs His heavenly army of angels to bring warnings of danger, tidings of joy, and messages of peace. The Bible calls them "ministering spirits sent to serve those who will inherit salvation" (Hebrews 1:14). Believing that God will send these angelic comforters to escort us out of this world and into the next should give great peace to our souls. The Bible says, "The Lord . . . shall preserve your soul . . . [He] shall preserve your going out and your coming in" (Psalm 121:7–8 NKJV).

We must remember, however, that while God's angels provide comfort and protection—even at death—it is God who dispatches them, and we are not to worship them.

For example, consider the exchange between John and an angel in Revelation. The apostle was so overwhelmed with the grandeur of Heaven that he fell at the feet of the angel to worship him. The angel spoke and said, "Do not do that! For I am your fellow servant, and of your brethren the prophets and of those who keep the words of this book. Worship God" (Revelation 22:9 NKJV). Scripture clearly condemns the worship of angels (Colossians 2:18). Only God—Father, Son, and Holy Spirit—is worthy of our praise and worship.

What is Jesus' role in Heaven?

--- ❋ ---

Christ is seated at the right hand of God in Heaven, where He is interceding on our behalf.

What exactly does this mean? The Bible says that God appointed His only Son, Jesus, as heir of all things, and when "He had by Himself purged our sins, sat down at the right hand of the Majesty on high" (Hebrews 1:3 NKJV) as our High Priest and Advocate. The Bible says, "We have one who speaks to the Father in our defense" (1 John 2:1). We may slip into sin, but we won't slip out of His hand.

What a promise for believers! When one of His own stumbles, Jesus tells His Father, "He repented . . . and I have forgiven him." Or perhaps He says, "Father, that dear lady belongs to Me; her sins are covered by My blood." Jesus is the heir of Heaven, and as His children we are "heirs of God and co-heirs with Christ" (Romans 8:17).

Jesus prayed, "I have given them the glory that you gave me. . . . May they be brought to complete unity to let the world know that you sent me" (John 17:22–23). While Christ reserves our place in Heaven, our eternal life was won through His work at Calvary. Our acceptance in Heaven, then, must be determined on earth, through repenting of sin and receiving Christ as our Savior and Lord.

From Heaven, the Lord also observes what is happening on earth. Just before Stephen died, "[he] looked up to heaven and saw the glory of God, and Jesus standing at the right hand of God. 'Look!' he said, 'I see heaven open and the Son of Man standing at the right hand of God.'" Stephen's accusers heard him say, "Lord Jesus, receive my spirit" (Acts 7:55–59). Stephen fell to the ground under the barrage of stones and cried, "'Lord, do not hold this sin against them.' . . . [Then] he fell asleep" (v. 60).

What conversation there must have been between Father and Son. No book is large enough to give a full account of Jesus' work (John 21:25). What matters most is that His work is complete, and our role in Heaven will be to glorify Him for what He has accomplished. We will marvel when we hear the rest of *His story*.

What are the benefits of death to believers?

━━━━━━━━ ✦ ━━━━━━━━

The greatest benefit is that we will be free from all the pains and sorrows and evils of this life, and we will be safely in God's presence forever.

When we purchase life insurance, the benefit package determines the cost of the policy, and the insured must die in order for the life insurance policy to be paid. If you think about it, the same sort of transaction occurred at Calvary, where Jesus was crucified. No matter how wealthy a person may be, only One could pay the cost of eternal life, and the benefits are guaranteed and held in the treasury of hope. The policy owner is the Lord Jesus Christ; the cost was His life's blood to redeem us from sin; the fully paid benefit is our assurance of eternal life in God's kingdom, redeemable to those who exchange a sinful heart for a forgiven heart. When those souls pass from death to new life, the faith of the things they hoped for is clearly seen: "Where your treasure is, there your heart will be also" (Luke 12:34).

God outlines His benefit package in *His will* for us:

- "My Father's will is that everyone who looks to the Son and believes in him shall have eternal life, and *I will* raise him up" (John 6:40, emphasis added).
- "He who loves me will be loved by my Father, and *I too will* love him and show myself to him" (John 14:21, emphasis added).
- "*I will* give the right to eat from the tree of life, which is in the paradise of God" (Revelation 2:7, emphasis added).
- "*I will* give you the crown of life" (Revelation 2:10, emphasis added).
- "*I will* write on him the name of my God" (Revelation 3:12, emphasis added).
- "*I will* give to drink without cost from the spring of the water of life" (Revelation 21:6, emphasis added).

- "He who overcomes will inherit all this, and *I will* be his God and he will be my son" (Revelation 21:7, emphasis added).

So, unlike the insurance policies *we* purchase, the greatest benefit received at a believer's death is not found in the small print, but in the nail prints in Jesus' hands.

Does God forbid cremation?

———— ✹ ————

S cripture teaches that we are to honor the body because it is the temple of the Holy Spirit (1 Corinthians 6:19). In Bible times, burial was the common practice because it was seen as a sign of respect. When cremation was practiced, it showed contempt for the person (Joshua 7:25). Today, cremation is often practiced in cultures that have no respect for the human body as God's creation, which usually leads Christians in those societies to reject cremation. God gave us our bodies, and when He saw all He had made, "it was very good" (Genesis 1:31).

While cremation is becoming more accepted among Christians today, burial (laying a body to rest in the earth) has been the preferred method as an act of respect for God's creation. It also reflects the great care that was given to the Lord's body after His death. Jesus said, "This is My body which is broken for you" (1 Corinthians 11:24 NKJV). Our hearts are touched when we read in

Scripture how the women went to the tomb on that first Easter morning hoping to anoint His body, only to find the tomb empty and an angel announcing His resurrection (Mark 16:1–7). One day we will stand before the Lord in Heaven, for our bodies also will be resurrected.

This doesn't mean that bodies disposed of in other ways—whether buried at sea, burned as martyrs at the stake, or human ashes scattered across hills and valleys—won't also be resurrected. The Bible says, "He will send his angels" to gather all people "from the four winds, from the farthest part of earth to the farthest part of heaven" (Mark 13:27 NKJV). Abraham said, "I am nothing but dust and ashes" (Genesis 18:27). The Bible tells us "the first man was of the dust of the earth" (1 Corinthians 15:47).

We should honor the earthly tent of our dwelling when it is in our power to do so, for the physical body is the work of His hands. But take comfort that God is able to bring together whatever has been scattered.

What does it mean to be "changed in the twinkling of an eye"?

I n the Greek language, the *twinkling of an eye* implies only half a wink—and that is the expression Paul used to describe how quickly God will transform our bodies at the resurrection.

In the computer age, users do not question the nanosecond (one billionth of a second), the unit of time it often takes a computer to access its memory. A person can begin to type a phrase and before he or she is finished, it will appear on the screen—yet many people doubt that God can transform His creation in the twinkling of an eye.

The Bible tells us that, at the end of the present age, one generation of believers will never know bodily death—namely, the generation that is still alive when Christ returns for His own. Jesus told the disciples during their last hours together before His death that He was going away. He then said, "I will come back and take you to be with me" (John 14:3). This event is called the Rapture.

They will then join with believers from throughout the ages in the final resurrection—the instant when our mortal bodies will be transformed into the likeness of our resurrected Lord Jesus Christ. Paul says, "Listen, I tell you a mystery: We will not all sleep, but we will all be changed—in a flash, in the twinkling of an eye, at the last trumpet. For the trumpet will sound, the dead will be raised imperishable, and we will be changed" (1 Corinthians 15:51–52).

The dust that returned to the earth in death will become Heaven-bound life with Christ—in the twinkling of an eye.

What is a resurrected body?

———————— ✵ ————————

Resurrected bodies are physical bodies reunited with the spirit (soul)—but without any imperfection or weakness. As such, they will be like the resurrected body of our Lord Jesus Christ.

At the resurrection, the fleshly, physical body that was prone to wander in sin will become a glorious, spirit-filled body set free from sin: "Just as we have borne the likeness of the earthly man, so shall we bear the likeness of the man from heaven [Christ]. . . . For the perishable must clothe itself with the imperishable, and the mortal with immortality" (1 Corinthians 15:49, 53).

The body that lies decaying in the grave may have been worn out with age, abused by disease or harm, or broken by an accident, but in the resurrection that body will be raised in glory! Our limited minds cannot begin to fathom what will transpire in that moment, but we do know that our resurrected bodies will be free of all infirmities and will know nothing of physical weakness. Limitations imposed on this earth are not known in Heaven. We will have a habitation from God that is incorruptible, immortal, and powerful, having been "sown in dishonor . . . raised in glory . . . sown in weakness . . . raised in power" (1 Corinthians 15:43). We may not be able to comprehend this now, but our bodies and our minds (our understanding) will be illuminated by Christ.

Scripture does not teach that we will be given a second body, but a new body—the same body that we walked around in on earth, only transformed, bearing the likeness of Christ. We don't have that kind of body now, but the old will pass away and the new will come (2 Corinthians 5:17). This principle, applied to the sinner's new life at the time of salvation, also looks forward to our new life in Heaven. Sin is defeated by Christ's sacrifice, and death is defeated by Christ's resurrection. The promise of eternal life on earth is fulfilled in the reality of Heaven.

Who will be included in the resurrection of the dead?

———— ✦ ————

Jesus taught that both the righteous and the un-righteous will be resurrected. When Jesus spoke to those who were persecuting Him, He said, "A time is coming when all who are in their graves will hear his voice and come out—those who have done good will rise to live, and those who have done evil will rise to be condemned" (John 5:28–29). Those who have received Christ will live with Him forever. Those who rejected Christ will live in eternity separated from Him. This is a grim reality.

But God's grace is also a reality. Christ died for *all* sinners (2 Corinthians 5:15). The Bible says that "he was despised and rejected by men" (Isaiah 53:3), but in His grace He desires that *all* receive the salvation extended to them by His outstretched arms on the cross.

Death is not the end for anyone, no matter who we

are. We live on—in Heaven with God or in that place of absolute hopelessness the Bible calls Hell. It is unbelief that shuts the door to Heaven and opens the one to Hell. It is unbelief that rejects the Word of God and refuses Christ as Savior. It is unbelief that causes men to turn deaf ears to the gospel. Only one answer will give a person the certain privilege of entering Heaven: "I have believed in Jesus Christ and accepted Him as my Savior." These are the bodies that will be raised in glory, power, and victory.

What is purgatory, and are some people sent there before they enter Heaven?

———— ✤ ————

Scripture gives no account of, and does not support the idea of, purgatory. The idea developed in medieval times, and the purpose was to designate a place where those who had died were sent to be purified from sin. But this would discount the work of Christ on the cross! The Bible says, "When you were dead in your sins . . . God made you alive with Christ. He forgave us *all* our sins" (Colossians 2:13, emphasis added).

The apostle Paul, under the direction of the Holy Spirit, wrote, "But God demonstrates his own love for us in this: While we were still sinners, Christ died for us. Since we have now been justified by his blood, how much more shall we be saved from God's wrath through him!" (Romans 5:8–9).

God's wrath toward sin has been satisfied—fully and completely—on the cross. "This Man [Jesus] . . . offered one sacrifice for sins forever. . . . For by one offering He has perfected forever those who are being sanctified" (Hebrews 10:12, 14 NKJV). Nothing can make us more righteous in God's sight than we already are, through the cleansing blood of Jesus Christ. By His death and resurrection He purchased our salvation—fully and completely.

Why would a loving God send anyone to Hell?

———————— ✹ ————————

If you think about it, people actually send themselves to Hell through their rebellion and unbelief in Jesus Christ. But let me assure you: God doesn't want us to go there.

The subject of Heaven is much easier for us to accept than the subject of Hell—yet the Bible teaches both. It may surprise you to discover that no one taught about or warned us against Hell more than Jesus—and we should take His words very seriously.

Some teach that everyone will eventually be saved, because a God of love would never send anyone to Hell. They contend that words like *eternal* and *everlasting* do not actually mean *forever*. However, the same word in the Bible that speaks of eternal banishment from God in Hell is also used to describe the eternal bliss of Heaven.

What is Hell? The Bible gives us several vivid images, such as calling it a place of "darkness, where there will be weeping and gnashing of teeth" (Matthew 8:12). It also says Hell is a place of absolute hopelessness, because God is absent from it, and those who go there will never experience Heaven's joy, beauty, and peace. Its inhabitants will be "shut out from the presence of the Lord and from the majesty of his power" (2 Thessalonians 1:9).

Not one word about Hell in the Bible would ever make us want to go there. A seminary professor once said, "Never preach about Hell without tears in your eyes." Don't take Hell lightly or talk yourself into believing it doesn't exist—it does.

Life on earth has two paths, two doors, and two destinations. Choose the only path that leads to the door of Heaven. Jesus said, "I am the way" (John 14:6); Jesus said, "I am the gate" (John 10:9); and He also said, "Repent, for the kingdom of heaven is near" (Matthew 4:17). He was thinking of you when He stepped out of Heaven. He considered your soul when He went to the cross. Jesus cares for you as He looks down from Heaven. Ask Him to come into your heart so that you may dwell with Him throughout eternity.

Do we become angels when we die, as some think?

———————— ✦ ————————

Although this may be an intriguing thought, we do not become angels when we die. Angels are different from us, and in Heaven that difference will be preserved.

The holy angels are glorious spiritual beings under the command of God, but the gift of grace has been extended to the human race. God made provision for the salvation of fallen men, but He made no provision for the salvation of the fallen angels, who rebelled against their Creator and followed Lucifer (or Satan). The holy angels, however, did not sin and they never lost their original glory or their relationship with God. This assures them of their exalted place in God's order—and even now they serve God with great power. The Bible says, "they are ministering spirits sent to serve those who will inherit salvation?" (Hebrews 1:14).

Jesus identified Himself with fallen humanity when He was "made a little lower than the angels" (Hebrews 2:9). Angels cannot testify of salvation by grace through faith, but they do exalt the One who stepped down from His throne of glory and onto the world's stage, humbling Himself in the sight of the angelic host. The Bible says, "Even angels long to look into these things" (1 Peter 1:12).

In Heaven, those whose souls have been redeemed by the bloodshed of Christ will serve Him with gladness and will in turn be served by God's holy angels. The angels will stand aside when believers are introduced to their boundless, eternal riches. If you think about it, no sinner saved by grace would ever want to give up his exalted position in Christ by becoming an angel.

The church is the body of Christ, and it represents the highest expression of God's love. No love could go deeper, rise higher, or extend farther than the amazing love that moved Him to give His only begotten Son to redeem the lost. And angels celebrate each one who is found: Jesus said, "I tell you, there is rejoicing in the presence of the angels of God over one sinner who repents" (Luke 15:10).

What Will We Do in Heaven?

With your blood you purchased
men for God from every tribe and
language and people and nation. You
have made them to be a kingdom
and priests to serve our God, and
they will reign on the earth.

—*Revelation 5:9–10*

What will we look like when we get to Heaven?

———————— ✸ ————————

The Bible doesn't answer all our questions about Heaven. However, this question is put to rest—at least in part—in 1 John 3:2: "What we will be has not yet been made known. But we know that when he appears, we shall be like him, for we shall see him as he is."

It is only natural to be curious about *what we do not know*. We long to know what is over the hill. Many have searched the Scriptures for a hint of what our bodies will look like in the afterlife.

What we'll look like in Heaven isn't stated in the Bible, but it seems that we will recognize one another, just as Moses and Elijah were recognized by the disciples who were witnesses of Jesus' transfiguration (Matthew 17:1–8). The Bible says "for the LORD does not see as man sees; for man looks at the outward appearance, but the LORD looks at the heart" (1 Samuel 16:7 NKJV).

Part of Heaven's glory is that our bodies will be transformed, and we will become like Jesus Christ in His perfect resurrected body. We won't be subject to the ills and ravages of old age like we are now, for we will be changed.

Only God could take two eyes, a nose, and a mouth, and make every person who has ever lived an individual—totally unique. It's not inconceivable, then, that God in Heaven can perfect His children—who bear His image—without changing their individual uniqueness.

While the Bible doesn't say exactly what we'll look like, it does tell us that our faces will reflect the face of our Redeemer. "[We] will see Your face in righteousness; [we] shall be satisfied when [we] awake in Your likeness" (Psalm 17:15 NKJV). Heaven will not reflect our earthly desires; instead we will reflect Heaven's King, our Lord Jesus Christ.

Will we sing with the angels in Heaven?

———— ✻ ————

Yes, we will sing in Heaven, and we will even hear Jesus sing (Zephaniah 3:17). Jesus promises, "In the presence of the congregation I will sing your praises" (Hebrews 2:12).

In the last book of the Bible, John saw in Heaven those who "held harps given them by God and sang the song of Moses . . . and the song of the Lamb" (Revelation 15:2–3). He also heard the angels singing in Heaven: "Then I looked and heard the voice of many angels, numbering thousands upon thousands, and ten thousand times ten thousand. They encircled the throne and . . . sang: 'Worthy is the Lamb'" (Revelation 5:11–12).

Singing is first mentioned in Exodus 15:1 when Moses and the children of Israel sang praises to the Lord for their deliverance from slavery. Later the Lord gave Moses a song, in praise of God's faithfulness to His

Word, and commanded him to teach it to the nation (Deuteronomy 31:19). In Heaven, we will sing songs of praise and thanksgiving to God for His greatness, goodness, and faithfulness.

Music is the universal language for the human race because it transcends the language barriers between us. John certainly grasped this when he heard singing in Heaven. Many dying believers have testified that they heard the music of Heaven. The Bible says, "Your dead shall live . . . they shall arise. Awake and sing" (Isaiah 26:19 NKJV).

Imagine the disciples singing with Jesus in the Upper Room on that fateful last night before His crucifixion. Scripture says they "sung a hymn" and then went to the Mount of Olives (Matthew 26:30). Psalms is called the hymnbook of the Bible, and many scholars believe the Lord would have chosen Psalm 118, traditionally sung by the Jews at Passover. Perhaps the angels will stand back when the saints sing, "You have become my salvation" (Psalm 118:21) and then join with our voices in proclaiming, "Give thanks to the LORD, for he is good; His love endures forever" (Psalm 118:1–2).

The prospect of singing with angels is inspiring, but singing with Jesus—and hearing Him sing—will be heavenly.

Will we be limited to one place in Heaven, or will we be able to travel?

———— ✷ ————

To say that we will be "confined" to Heaven would indicate that there is something more . . . something still missing. The Bible's promise to us is that Jesus will be there to welcome us into His inexpressible splendor and we will be satisfied. If we are satisfied, then we will not want anything more (Psalm 17:15). "I have placed before you an open door that no one can shut" (Revelation 3:8). Heaven's gates will never be shut (Revelation 21:25). Jesus said, "It is your Father's good pleasure to give you the kingdom" (Luke 12:32 NKJV).

We would have a small faith if we believed that God's work among His people would be diminished in Heaven compared to what He did among us on earth. "Can you search out the deep things of God? Can you find out the limits of the Almighty? They are higher than heaven" (Job 11:7 NKJV). The Bible speaks of "heaven and the heaven of heavens [that] cannot contain God" (1 Kings 8:27 NKJV). The psalmist said, "Such knowledge is too wonderful for me. . . . I cannot attain it" (Psalm 139:6 NKJV). When we get to Heaven, we will be in His presence forever. Jesus said, "Where I am, there you may be also" (John 14:3 NKJV). Our earthly minds are limited, but when we move to God's country, our understanding will be illuminated. We will not want to leave because His glory will take eternity to explore.

In Heaven, our knowledge will be perfect—and so will all creation. "Creation itself will be liberated from its bondage to decay and brought into the glorious freedom of the children of God" (Romans 8:21). Will we ride on chariots of clouds or walk on the wings of the wind like the Lord? (Psalm 104:3).

We don't know the scope of our activity in Heaven, but Jesus promised that we would be with Him. Stop and consider this wondrous God.

Will we see people in Heaven we couldn't get along with on earth?

———————— ✸ ————————

We'll not only see them, but we'll get along with them perfectly. In Heaven, the past will be forgiven; they will be perfect—and so will we!

God's forgiveness means the complete blotting out of the dirt and degradation of our past, present, *and future*. This is our hope in Christ—that we are made new through Him. That process begins when we surrender our lives to Jesus Christ (2 Corinthians 5:17)—and it will be perfected in Heaven. "You have come to . . . the city of the living God . . . to the spirits of righteous men made perfect" (Hebrews 12:22–23).

An unforgiving spirit holds a grudge against someone who has offended us. Some people just naturally rub us the wrong way, just as we rub some people the wrong way. But how will we feel when we meet them in Heaven? Paul reminds us that in a flash, we will be changed (1 Corinthians 15:51–55).

In the meantime, it's impossible to be at peace with ourselves and with others if we have an unforgiving heart, which is a sin. The Bible says, "Everyone who has this hope in [Christ] purifies himself, just as [Christ] is pure" (1 John 3:3).

Guilt and unforgiving feelings are the focal point of much psychiatric counseling. So tremendous is the weight of our guilt that the great and glorious truth of God's forgiveness should encourage every believer in Jesus Christ. God's goodness in forgiving us means even more when we realize that—through faith in Christ— we are without guilt in God's sight; we are clothed forever with Christ's righteousness. The only reason our sins can be forgiven is because Jesus Christ paid their full penalty on the cross.

The Bible tells us that a sinful mind is hostile to God (Romans 8:7), but in Heaven we will have total peace (Luke 19:38). We will be *completely* changed when we get to Heaven—and so, too, will those we couldn't get along with while on earth.

If God can make the lion and the lamb lie down together, we can trust Him to take care of our fractured relationships as we enter our heavenly home.

Will there be marriage in Heaven?

———— ✿ ————

Marriage in Heaven will be on a much higher plane because the church will be united with Christ.

Marriage is the first institution God gave on earth, and it is a wonderful relationship. He provided this special union to alleviate loneliness (Genesis 2:18) and for the purpose of populating the earth (Genesis 9:7). In Heaven, there will be no loneliness—fellowship will be more than the human mind can understand, and Heaven will be populated by the saints born of God.

When Jesus was asked about marriage in Heaven by those who did not believe in the resurrection, He said, "When the dead rise, they will neither marry nor be given in marriage; they will be like the angels in heaven" (Mark 12:25). This does not mean that the resurrected will become angels, but instead refers specifically to the fact that angels are not married and do not procreate.

Heavenly marriage is Christ's special relationship

with those He purchased with His blood. "For your Maker is your husband" (Isaiah 54:5); "I will betroth you to me forever . . . in righteousness and justice, in love and compassion. I will betroth you in faithfulness, and you will acknowledge the LORD" (Hosea 2:19–20). The earthbound mind is not capable of realizing the greater bond with Almighty God, but in Heaven every carnal thought will fall away.

While we cannot fathom not knowing our spouses or children in the earthly sense, Jesus tells us not to worry about these things. "A time is coming when I will no longer use this kind of language . . . I have told you these things, so that in me you may have peace. . . . Take heart! I have overcome the world" (John 16:25, 33). Marriage as we know it in its human form will not be practiced in Heaven because it will be perfected in the Lord Jesus Christ.

Although our human minds cannot fully understand heavenly things, the day is coming when we will comprehend all great truths—including this one.

Will we grieve for lost loved ones when we are in Heaven?

━━━━━━━━ ✦ ━━━━━━━━

In God's glorious presence, all our concerns and griefs will be erased.

It's hard to imagine how we can be happy if our loved ones aren't in Heaven because of their unbelief, but Scripture assures that "even the memory of them will disappear" (Psalm 9:6 TLB). God's plan will be revealed, in all of its fullness, in Heaven. Our present understanding is limited, but one day we will comprehend the perfection of His justice and mercy: "The former things will not be remembered, nor will they come to mind. . . . Be glad and rejoice" (Isaiah 65:17–18).

The human mind has but a wisp of understanding. As believers, through the work of the Holy Spirit, our faith grows deeper concerning the things of God. He first gives us faith to believe in Him, then our faith and knowledge of His Word grow so we understand that He can and will do all things well. He demonstrated this by giving His life as a ransom for many (Mark 10:45).

Paul says, "Now I know in part; then I shall know fully, even as I am fully known. And now these three remain: faith, hope, and love. But the greatest of these is love" (1 Corinthians 13:12–13). We must have these three gifts from God to live for Him on earth. In Heaven, our faith will be complete, for we will see Him face-to-face. In Heaven, our hope will become reality, for we will no longer have to patiently endure before being fully in His presence. And the love that He exhibited for us on earth and instilled in us to love Him and others will continue forever, because God is love (1 John 4:8).

The scope of God's love will not be fully realized until it is revealed in Heaven. The mystery of God's love would not be a mystery if we knew all the answers. All our concern, worry, and grief will come to an end when we begin new life in Heaven.

Will we receive an inheritance in Heaven?

———— ✷ ————

The Bible promises that in Heaven we will receive a glorious inheritance—the inheritance of eternal life in all its fullness.

Can you imagine answering a knock on your door to find someone notifying you that you had inherited a kingdom? It is inconceivable. But for the believer in Jesus, this is exactly what happens when you open the door of your heart and invite Christ to come inside and dwell within you. He promises to share the wealth of His riches, power, and glory with you.

My late wife, Ruth, had a beautiful, antique chest inlaid with rare pieces of wood that her grandfather had built years ago. When visitors asked where she got it, she answered with pride, "I inherited it."

Inheritance is a biblical truth, (mentioned over

two hundred times), that will be fulfilled completely in Heaven. God has chosen us to be His own inheritance—His very own people (Psalm 33:12). He has also chosen "our inheritance for us" (Psalm 47:4). Heirloom chests can burn in a few minutes, but we will receive "an inheritance that can never perish, spoil or fade—kept in heaven for you" (1 Peter 1:4).

God told the priests of Israel that they would not inherit any land—for *He* would be their inheritance (Ezekiel 44:28). This was looking forward to the New Testament promise that Christ's church—a holy priesthood—would inherit eternal life in Christ.

The book of Ephesians speaks specifically about the inheritance we can look forward to in Heaven: the "unsearchable riches" of God's grace (3:8); "his glorious riches" (v. 16); and "his incomparably great power" (v. 19).

The things we inherit on earth may be a great blessing—or a terrible curse. Countless lives have been ruined by riches left to irresponsible heirs. However, as children of the King, our inheritance will not spoil, nor will it spoil us. Let's give "thanks to the Father, who has qualified [us] to share in the inheritance" (Colossians 1:12). What a wonderful promise!

Will we be judged in Heaven or receive rewards in Heaven?

———— ✸ ————

At the judgment seat of Christ, believers will receive rewards—not the reward of eternal life, for that has already been given to them, but of other blessings God has for us.

The apostle Paul compared this to an athletic contest in which the victor would appear before a judge who would determine his reward, not his punishment. We can understand this when we think of the Olympics. Athletes compete for a prize. Some receive bronze medals; others, silver; and first-place winners receive the gold. This is the thought behind the judgment seat in Heaven.

Believers will not be judged for their sin, for Christ dealt with our sin on the cross at Calvary. Instead, at the judgment seat, our work on earth for Christ's Kingdom will be evaluated and rewarded according to God's perfect righteousness and justice.

The fact that we can stand before Him at all is a miracle of His grace in our lives. Then, what we do in obedience and by the strength of the Holy Spirit will be evaluated, and "each will be rewarded according to his own labor. For we are God's fellow workers; you are God's field, God's building" (1 Corinthians 3:8–9). This is a tremendous incentive to work for the Lord, with the right motive in our hearts. We won't all receive the same rewards. We do not have the same abilities, but we will be judged according to our faithful response to the gifts and opportunities given to us.

And it's not just the work of reaching out to those in need of the gospel, but also how we conduct ourselves in body and mind (2 Peter 3:11). God's rewards are incentives for us to live a holy life of faithful service to Christ—not to others—during our time on earth. These rewards are described as *crowns*, as we see in Paul's letter to Timothy: "I have fought the good fight. . . . There is laid up for me the crown of righteousness, which the Lord, the righteous Judge, will give to me on that Day, and not to me only but also to all who have loved His appearing" (2 Timothy 4:7–8 NKJV).

Jesus said, "Rejoice and be glad, because great is your reward in heaven" (Matthew 5:12). Then He gave us a remarkable promise: "Behold, I am coming soon! My reward is with me, and I will give to everyone according to what he has done" (Revelation 22:12). The greatest reward of all will be to hear our Lord saying, "Well done, good and faithful servant!" (Matthew 25:23).

Do people who have died and gone to Heaven know what is going on down here on earth?

———— ✦ ————

Heaven will be glorious. We will meet the saints of old. There we will walk the streets of gold and be reunited with those we love. When we enter Heaven, we will have crossed the finish line to meet the One who will reveal stories yet untold.

Consider the scene in Hebrews 12:1 describing the heroes of the faith who are now in Heaven: "Since we are surrounded by such a great cloud of witnesses . . . let us run with perseverance the race marked out for us." While we aren't given any detail, the previous chapter in Hebrews gives us examples of that *great cloud of witnesses*—the saints of old who ran the race of faith and finished well. We draw strength from their victorious finish on earth, bearing testimony to their faith in God and God's faithfulness to them.

Absolutely nothing can be hidden from Him. The Bible does not tell us if the souls in God's presence know what is happening on earth. What it does tell us is that God knows what is happening in our lives. Our desire as believers should not be to please men (Galatians 1:10), but to run the race to please God: "My eyes are fixed on you, [O Lord]" (Psalm 141:8). And Jesus Christ watches our every move and knows our every thought. How thankful we should be, for He is our strength: "The eyes of the Lord range throughout the earth to strengthen those whose hearts are fully committed to him" (2 Chronicles 16:9).

Do we welcome the eyes of the Lord? Do we live each day knowing that the Lord of Heaven looks down on us? He is not waiting for us to stumble, but He is there when we do. He is seeking our loyalty to Him: "Whatever you do, work at it with all your heart, as working for the Lord, not for men, since you know that you will receive an inheritance from the Lord as a reward. It is the Lord Christ you are serving" (Colossians 3:23–24).

Can We Be Sure We Will Go to Heaven?

And this is the testimony: God has
given us eternal life, and this life is
in his Son. He who has the Son has
life; he who does not have the Son of
God does not have life.

—1 John 5:11–12

How good do we have to be to get into Heaven?

--------- ✳ ---------

The answer may shock you—but the truth is that we will never be good enough to go to Heaven on our own.

Why is this? The reason is because God is absolutely pure and holy, and no evil can ever enter *His* home. Just one sin will keep us away from His presence—and no one can claim to be sinless. We are born in sin (Romans 5:12); we are sinners by nature. The Bible says, "For all have sinned and fall short of the glory of God" (Romans 3:23).

God doesn't take our good deeds and bad deeds and weigh them against each other; if He did, He'd be letting us into Heaven with our sins. God's standard is nothing less than perfection. We may think we're good enough—but if so, we are filled with pride, which is a sin. The Bible says, "If we claim to be without sin, we deceive ourselves and the truth is not in us" (1 John 1:8). But Jesus preached repentance to receive eternal life in Heaven (Mark 1:15), and it is through His shed blood that our sins are forgiven, covered by His goodness, and this is why those who believe in Him will be received into Heaven.

Suppose you had a barrel of water and it had been filtered and distilled until no impurities remained. If someone asked you to drink it, you wouldn't hesitate. But suppose someone put a drop of raw sewage in it. Would you drink it? Of course not. The same is true with sin.

This is why God sent His Son, the Lord Jesus Christ, to earth to redeem us by His love and His sacrifice. Jesus was without sin because He was God in human flesh—but on the cross all our sins were transferred to Him, and He took the judgment we deserve.

Don't trust in yourself and your good works, but turn to Jesus and trust Him alone for your salvation. It is *the* life-changing decision that will settle once and for all your place in Heaven. Don't miss what the Lord has in store for those who love Him and are willing to let Him be the Master of their lives.

How did Jesus' death make it possible for us to go to Heaven?

———— ✦ ————

B y His death Jesus paid the penalty for our sins. This alone gives us everlasting life with Him in Heaven.

We are so used to sin that we easily forget just how serious it is in the eyes of God. Every sin we commit is an act of rebellion—a deliberate renunciation of God's rightful authority over us. But sin is serious for another reason: it ravages our souls, bringing heartache and brokenness into our lives. Most of all, it cuts us off from fellowship with God.

Because of God's great love for us, however, He provided the way for us to be forgiven and cleansed of our sins—and, ultimately, to spend eternity with Him. We could never cleanse ourselves; sin's stain is too deep. But God made our forgiveness possible by sending Jesus Christ into the world as the final and complete sacrifice for our sins. On the cross, Jesus took the divine judgment that you and I deserve. He died in our place. The Bible says, "For Christ died for sins once for all, the righteous for the unrighteous, to bring you to God" (1 Peter 3:18).

Do you want freedom from sin's penalty? Believe that Christ died *for you*. He suffered *for you*. He won the battle over sin *for you*. He rose from the grave and was victorious over death so that *you* can live forever. But you must respond by receiving Him into your heart by faith and by committing your life to Him without reserve. He is waiting for you to confess your sins, to surrender yourself to Him, and to make Him Lord and Master of your life. He is preparing a place in Heaven for all those who will come to Him in faith and complete submission. Don't delay. Make sure of your salvation by turning your life over to Him now.

What is the Book of Life and does it really exist?

━━━━━━ ✷ ━━━━━━

The Book of Life is God's record of all those over the centuries who have trusted Christ as their Savior and have followed Him as Lord.

Many books are mentioned in the Bible: the Book of the Covenant, Book of the Law, Book of the Kings, Book of the Records, Book of Remembrance, Book of the Lord, and so forth. But one book is supremely important: the Book of Life. The Bible says that in God's presence "books were opened. Another book was opened, which is the book of life. . . . Only those whose names are written in the Lamb's book of life" will enter Heaven (Revelation 20:12, 21:27).

If you have given your life to Christ, your name is already written there. Furthermore, Jesus has promised that if you belong to Him, nothing will ever be able to remove your name from its pages. He declared, "I will never blot out his name from the Book of Life, but will acknowledge his name before my Father and his angels" (Revelation 3:5). This promise should be written on the heart of every believer!

What about those who have not turned to Christ in repentance and faith, who have rejected Him as their Lord and Savior? Tragically, their names will not be found there, and they will enter eternity with no hope of Heaven. The Bible solemnly warns, "If anyone's name was not found written in the book of life, he was thrown into the lake of fire" (Revelation 20:15).

For anyone reading this who has not given his or her life to Christ, it's not too late! Now is the time to acknowledge your sin before God and accept His merciful love for you. Don't turn away. Pray to Him for forgiveness and, by faith, receive Jesus Christ into your life. Then you will have assurance that your name has been written in the Book of Life which God Himself will open and read someday. Nothing will bring us greater joy than hearing the Savior call our names.

Will people who claim to believe in Jesus and yet never show any signs of a changed life go to Heaven when they die?

———— ✻ ————

Only God knows people's hearts, and whether or not they honestly gave their life to Christ.

Jesus warned, however, that "not everyone who says to me, 'Lord, Lord,' shall enter the kingdom of heaven, but only he who does the will of my Father who is in heaven" (Matthew 7:21). No Christian is perfect, of course—but someday our true relationship with Christ will be revealed. The Bible warns, "Everything is uncovered and laid bare before the eyes of him to whom we must give account" (Hebrews 4:13).

Nevertheless, one of the signs of a true Christian is a changed life. In fact, if there is no indication that a person wants to follow Christ, it strongly suggests that their faith may not be sincere and they may not be saved. The Bible compares a person like this to a corpse—physically present but lifeless (James 2:26). This is a sobering truth.

We must not deceive ourselves into thinking that we will be saved if we haven't truly trusted Christ as Savior and aren't seeking to follow Him as Lord. "By their fruit you will recognize them" (Matthew 7:20). One day Christ will acknowledge to His Father in Heaven those who belong to Him and have demonstrated the fruit of His Spirit.

Are you seeking to follow Christ in every area of your life—with His help? It is the only way to live victoriously.

What are some of the signs of a changed life?

———— ✹ ————

Christ calls us to live lives that reflect His character of righteousness and love. The Bible says, "Now that you have been set free from sin . . . the benefit you reap leads to holiness, and the result is eternal life" (Romans 6:22).

As we submit our lives to Jesus Christ, His Holy Spirit begins changing us from within. Our hearts begin to reflect the love of God, and our minds begin to think on a higher plane—a spiritual plane—that leads us to godly action.

Jesus said, "I was thirsty and you gave me something to drink, I was a stranger and you invited me in, I needed clothes and you clothed me, I was sick and you looked after me, I was in prison and you came to visit me" (Matthew 25:35–36). Many people demonstrate good works toward others, but for those who follow the Lord

Jesus, their lives will reflect holiness of life, they'll have a desire to tell others what Christ has done for them, and they'll reach out with His love to others who are in need.

Scripture tells us how to live a life pleasing to the Lord: "Present your bodies a living sacrifice, holy, acceptable to God, which is your reasonable service. And do not be conformed to this world, but be transformed by the renewing of your mind, that you may prove what is that good and acceptable and perfect will of God" (Romans 12:1–2 NKJV). Living a godly life is the process of being "conformed to the likeness of his Son" (Romans 8:29). The true believer in the Lord Jesus Christ will mature spiritually through feeding on the Word of God. This is why the careful and obedient reading of the Bible is essential to living a godly life in the midst of an immoral world. Reading God's Word and meditating on its truth will have a purifying effect upon your mind and heart, and will be demonstrated in your life. Let nothing take the place of this daily privilege.

Can you repent for the first time just before you die and still go to Heaven?

————— ✵ —————

One of the Bible's greatest truths is that God stands ready to forgive us whenever we turn to Him in repentance and faith—even at the end of life. The Lord wants all people to come to repentance. The Bible says, "He is patient with you, not wanting anyone to perish, but everyone to come to repentance" (2 Peter 3:9).

The Bible repeatedly warns us, however, not to wait until the last minute. For one thing, we do not know what the future holds; life is uncertain. Death can snatch us from this world in an instant, before we could even cry out to God. If a person is dying of a heart attack and, out of fear, prays for God's salvation, is that repentance sincere? Only the Lord knows. My question for such a person would be this: If you didn't want anything to do with Christ while you were living, why would you want to spend eternity with Him?

But we do find an answer in Scripture for someone who is sincere of heart. When Jesus was hanging on the cross between two criminals, one mocked Jesus because He wouldn't save Himself. But the other turned to Jesus and, in faith, cried out, "Jesus, remember me when you come into your kingdom." Christ replied, "I tell you the truth, today you will be with me in paradise" (Luke 23:42–43). Although he had only a brief time to live, he received the gift of salvation.

The Bible says, "I tell you, now is the time of God's favor, now is the day of salvation" (2 Corinthians 6:2). Don't presume upon God's grace. Don't treat lightly Christ's death on the cross. Don't risk being flat on your back and looking up toward Heaven before answering the most important question that confronts you: *What will you do with Jesus?* Receive Him today.

Does God allow people into Heaven who are mentally handicapped and don't fully understand He loves them and accepts them just as they are?

———— ✦ ————

God has the pulse of eternal life in His hand, and He knows the limitations of each of us. None of us are saved because we understand everything there is to know about the heavenly Father, the Lord Jesus Christ, and the Holy Spirit. Salvation comes based on confessing sin and receiving God's gift of grace. Babies, young children, and the mentally handicapped cannot comprehend their limitations or the truths of God's plan of salvation—but God, in His grace, receives each of them just as they are and changes their hearts.

A tender passage in Scripture is when the little children gathered around Jesus. They didn't have any profound understanding of who He was or why He came, yet He welcomed them and told His disciples, "Let the little children come to me, and do not hinder them, for the kingdom of God belongs to such as these" (Mark 10:14).

God has much to teach us through infants and children with special needs. They are completely dependent on others; they must trust their caregivers for everything. There is a lesson for us when Jesus says that we must become as little children. He meant we must place our complete trust in Him, giving up our desires for His, and allow Him to direct our every step.

Scripture sheds light on this difficult subject. Solomon says that a stillborn child is better off than one who disregards his own life (Ecclesiastes 6:3 NKJV), and Job cursed the day he was born and said, "Why did I not perish at birth? . . . For now I would be lying down in peace; I would be asleep and at rest" (Job 3:11, 13).

If you have babies and handicapped children who have been taken from you by death, receive comfort in the sovereignty of the God of love. Commit to teaching others, who do have the capacity to understand the gospel, that God stands ready to cover our sin with His mercy and grace. Do not weep for those *in His care*, but for those who have not yet found that place of safety in the Savior's comforting love.

Does God forgive even murderers or others who have committed terrible crimes? Can they go to Heaven?

—————— ✦ ——————

G od's amazing love opens the way of salvation to all people who truly repent and put their faith and trust in Christ—even murderers.

We see this demonstrated in the transformation of the apostle Paul. Before his conversion, he hated Christians and was responsible for the death of some, as we see in his admission: "When the blood of your martyr Stephen was shed, I stood there giving my approval" (Acts 22:20). Remarkably, when Paul met Christ on the road to Damascus, the Lord forgave him fully and completely, and used him to spread the gospel throughout the Roman Empire.

Human life is sacred in God's eyes, and murdering someone is a terrible act—so terrible that the Old Testament decreed the murderer must pay for it with his life. One of the Ten Commandments declares, "You shall not murder" (Exodus 20:13).

Sin is sin. No matter who we are, the Bible says we all have sinned, and we all deserve God's judgment. But Jesus came to earth to rescue sinners: the liar and the lame, the murderer and the maimed. He came with the good news of redemption. His desire is that all would repent and call on Him. He wants to pull everyone—including the murderer—from Satan's clutches. There is no salvation without a Savior—and His name is Jesus. He came to save His people from their sins (Matthew 1:21).

If you were trapped in a house on fire, you wouldn't run from those snatching you from the flames. Don't resist the voice of the One who is calling your name. Even in the darkest moment, God is willing to shed light into the darkest soul.

What is meant by "broad is the road that leads to destruction, and many enter through it. But small is the gate and narrow the road that leads to life, and only a few find it" (Matthew 7:13–14)?

———— ✿ ————

Jesus was close to the end of His earthly life when He preached these words in the Sermon on the Mount. He was reminding His followers to turn their backs on sinful, self-centered ways of living and to start living in complete submission to Him. Jesus warned, "If anyone would come after me, he must deny himself and take up his cross daily and follow me" (Luke 9:23). This is hard for us to do—in fact, it's impossible without the help of the Holy Spirit. This is why Jesus promised that when He returned to His Father, He would send His Holy Spirit to help us in our weaknesses.

Many people refuse to let Christ take control of their

lives. It's not easy for human nature to give up control. We think we know what is best for us, but the human race has proven from the beginning its inability to live righteously.

Too often we are concerned with how much like this world we can become. We act as if it doesn't matter how we live. But God says we aren't to live worldly lives, but to live for Christ and bear witness of His truth to the world.

Refusing to seek God's will and live for Him will lead only to eternal destruction. Don't be misled by following what the crowd does—that's the broad way. Since Christ was willing to give His life for you, entrust your life to Him. He is the only One who knows where your life is going. No matter your plans, no matter your own will, His ways are better and His pathway will lead you to the better way. This is the narrow road—but it leads to Heaven.

Does anyone have the right to say who is and who isn't going to Heaven?

---　❋　---

Only God knows our hearts and He alone has the right to judge who is genuinely saved or lost. The Bible says, "he will judge the world in righteousness and the peoples in his truth" (Psalm 96:13).

God is the just and all-knowing judge, and we must never try to put ourselves in His place by saying that we know a particular person will be eternally lost or saved. None of us knows what happens between God and an individual. Even in the last breaths of life, someone can turn in faith to Christ and be saved.

A reporter for a national magazine once confessed, "My grandmother didn't accept Jesus as her Savior before she died, and she was the most perfect person I've ever known. I can't imagine eternity without my grandmother, so since she died without forgiveness of sin, I will not repent either because I want to spend eternity with the most wonderful person I've ever known." My colleague responded, "Then you've never met the Lord Jesus." She explained, "When you reach your eternal destination, you may find that your grandmother is in Heaven because in the last moments of life she may have called on the Lord and was miraculously saved. You will then find yourself eternally separated not only from your precious grandmother, but also from the most wonderful Person you could ever know."

We also should not presume that people will go to Heaven just because they claim to be a Christian. Matthew 7:21 says, "Not everyone who says to me, 'Lord, Lord,' will enter the kingdom of heaven, but only he who does the will of my Father who is in heaven." We must take seriously the Bible's admonition, "Examine yourselves to see whether you are in the faith" (2 Corinthians 13:5).

Don't fall into Satan's trap by comparing yourself to anyone else. Set your eyes instead on the One who died for you. Seek Him; He will save you. Live for Him; He will open up Heaven's door for you.

What did Jesus mean when He said, "The last will be first, and the first will be last" (Matthew 20:16)?

———— ✦ ————

J esus was pointing out the danger of thinking we will go to Heaven because we are prominent or religious. But our salvation is by grace alone.

In this passage (Matthew 20:1–16), Jesus told a parable about men who had been hired to work in a field. Some worked all day while others were given work late in the day—but both were given the same wage.

As we've seen with the thief on the cross who acknowledged his sinfulness to Jesus and was given eternal life in his last moments, the same joys of Heaven come to those saved early in life as those who are saved late in life. What true believer could possibly deny such joy to those who almost missed having their sins forgiven? It would break the heart of God for one of His own to derive joy from seeing people denied forgiveness of sin just because they waited until the last minute. The only sadness we should feel is that such a person missed out on walking with the Lord—on serving Him, witnessing for Him, enjoying His presence, and living life in obedience to His Lordship. We should do no less than the angels who rejoice when a sinner is received into the fellowship of God's eternal home, even if in the last mile of the way.

It is Jesus who gave His life as "a ransom for many" (Matthew 20:28). The first and the last will be welcomed into His presence with the same outcome—forgiveness and eternal life. Who are you praying for who may be clinging to the last moments of earthly life without Christ? May our prayer lists be filled with names, and may we pray diligently that the Holy Spirit would speak to their hearts.

Can Satan determine the destiny of a human soul?

———— ✦ ————

No, Satan cannot force anyone to follow him, nor can he determine the destiny of a human soul. When Jesus said, "Fear him who, after the killing of the body, has power to throw you into hell" (Luke 12:5), He was referring to God, not to Satan.

The Bible teaches us that each individual determines his or her eternal destiny, and it is God in His perfect righteousness who enacts judgment. Unbelief shuts the door to Heaven and opens it to Hell. Man condemns himself to eternal Hell because he refuses God's way of salvation and hope of eternal life with Him.

The same Book that tells us over and over again of God's love also warns us constantly of the devil who would come between us and God—the devil who is waiting to ensnare men's souls. Satan does not have authority in people's lives, but he does employ his powers to tempt us toward evil.

The closer you are to Christ, the farther away you are from the devil—so keep close to Jesus. We must be constantly aware that Satan can take any human effort and twist it to serve his own purposes; this is why we are told to beware of Satan's deception. Only God can thwart the plans of Satan and his legions.

The cross was designed to defeat Satan. If a man will not submit to Jesus Christ, then his life will be controlled by Satan. While Satan cannot snatch believers from the security of God's hand, he rejoices when we are inconsistent, because he knows that an inconsistent Christian is an ineffective Christian. But if you are in Christ, Satan has no ultimate power over you. I have yet to see Satan overcome a truly joyful, Spirit-filled Christian.

What if someone doesn't feel that God has forgiven him or isn't sure if he is saved, although he has asked Jesus to come into his life?

———— ✵ ————

God does not want us to be unsure of our salvation or filled with doubts about our eternal destiny.

Instead, He wants us to trust His promise that our sins have been forgiven and that we have been adopted into God's family and will spend eternity with Him. Jesus said, "Never will I leave you; never will I forsake you" (Hebrews 13:5). Don't trust your feelings—trust only God's Word.

Some have prayed insincerely that Jesus would come into their lives. Perhaps they were coaxed by a friend, or they were looking for an "experience." But if doubt comes to people who have sincerely believed Christ had saved them, the Bible says, "Examine yourselves to see whether you are in the faith; test yourselves. Do you not realize that Christ Jesus is in you—unless of course you fail the test?" (2 Corinthians 13:5).

The key is to trust God's promises. Remember: Satan can cast doubt in your mind if you've become distant in your relationship to the Lord. Or Satan may be trying to defeat the power of your testimony. Don't give Satan a foothold; the greatest roadblock to Satan's work is the Christian who, above all else, lives for God, walks with integrity, is filled with the Spirit, and is obedient to God's truth. The apostle John wrote, "This is the testimony: God has given us eternal life, and this life is in his Son; He who has the Son has life; . . . the evil one cannot harm him" (1 John 5:11–12, 18).

Feed on God's Word, pray, fellowship with other believers, and ask the Holy Spirit to strengthen your spiritual walk. God's promises can be trusted, because God cannot lie. And once you have trusted Christ, thank Him that your past is forgiven and your future is secure—solely because of Him.

What Difference
Does Heaven Make?

He must turn from evil and do good;
he must seek peace and pursue it.
For the eyes of the Lord are on the
righteous and his ears are attentive
to their prayer. . . . But even if you
should suffer for what is right, you
are blessed.

—1 Peter 3:11–12, 14

If Heaven is real, what difference should it make in our lives right now?

———— ✻ ————

The privilege of being in touch with Heaven right now greatly enhances our time on earth. Knowing Heaven is real, and that we will go there someday, makes a great difference in the way we live.

For one thing, Heaven gives us hope—hope for today and hope for the future. No matter what we're facing, we know it is only temporary, and ahead of us is Heaven. The Bible says, "Though outwardly we are wasting away . . . our light and momentary troubles are achieving for us an eternal glory that far outweighs them all" (2 Corinthians 4:16–17).

The Christian life is a joyful life. Christianity was never meant to make us miserable; the ministry of Jesus Christ was one of joy. The Bible teaches that a life of inward peace and outward victory is a Christian's birthright—and our certainty of Heaven makes this a reality.

The Lord Jesus has given us the spirit of joy as one of the marks of a true believer, to make our time on earth worthwhile, and to remind us to keep our eyes focused on the promise of Heaven.

Our certainty of Heaven also makes a difference because we are in touch with Heaven right now. Few people have ever had the honor of speaking with a king, much less visiting him in his kingdom. But as believers in Christ, we don't have to wait until we die to have an audience with the King of kings in Heaven. We have access to Him now—on earth.

When our hearts are surrendered totally to the will of God, then we delight in seeing Him use us in any way He pleases. Our prospects seem brighter when we're looking up for His direction. Our plans and desires begin to agree with His, and we accept His direction in our lives. Our sense of joy, satisfaction, and fulfillment in life increases no matter what the circumstances, if we are in the center of God's will. Every day we live has meaning and purpose.

Is the old quip true, that Christians are so heavenly minded they aren't any earthly good?

❋

No, it isn't true—because Christ has given us an earthly mission with a heavenly goal. The more seriously we take Heaven, the more seriously we'll take our responsibilities on earth.

Life is short; none of us knows how long we have. Live each day as if it were your last—for someday it will be. If you are ever going to live for Christ, it should be now.

Every day is a gift from God, and it isn't to be wasted or spent in selfish indulgence, but to be lived for Christ. There are so many professing Christians who walk hand in hand with the world making it difficult to distinguish between them and unbelievers. Those who have actually experienced daily fellowship with Christ, however, know that it surpasses all worldly activities. In His prayer for His disciples, Jesus said, "My prayer is not that you take them out of the world but that you protect them from the evil one. . . . Sanctify them by the truth" (John 17:15, 17).

Jesus doesn't call us to escape from this world and its problems, but to confront them with His power and love. We are to be involved in the world—but without being contaminated, influenced, or swayed by its ways. This distinction can be achieved only by a close walk with Christ, having the mind of Christ, and seeking the leadership of the Holy Spirit every hour of the day. To be heavenly-minded is the only way to do earthly good.

Why doesn't God take us to Heaven the minute we commit our lives to Christ?

━━━━━━ ❋ ━━━━━━

I f God were to take all those He immediately saves to Heaven, He would not be true to His Word. Jesus said, "As long as it is day, we must do the work of him who sent me. Night is coming, when no one can work" (John 9:4). This is the heavenly design for the body of Christ—the church. Jesus told His disciples, "By this my Father is glorified, that you bear much fruit and so prove to be my disciples" (John 15:8 ESV).

Earth isn't Heaven's waiting room where we idly sit until departure time. Earth is a dramatic stage displaying good and evil; Christ's victory over Satan's deception; Heaven's glory over the gore of Hell. We are part of this divine drama.

As long as we are on this earth, God's purpose is for us to bring honor and glory to Him by the way we live and work, so that we can win souls for His kingdom.

Without anyone left to demonstrate Christ's compassion and righteousness, what kind of world would it be? Without anyone left to tell others about God's love, how would people ever hear about Christ or put their trust in Him? The answer is obvious: our world would be condemned to perpetual spiritual darkness. Jesus' command to His disciples has never been revoked: "Go into all the world and preach the good news to all creation" (Mark 16:15).

I don't know anyone who looks forward to sitting for hours in a waiting room. Neither should we be content to sit idly waiting for Heaven. Instead we should be busy at work in the name of the Lord, so many others will join us on that heavenly journey home. We are all called to be witnesses for Christ, bringing His love and transforming power to a broken and confused world.

The Bible says that some day Christ will come back to rule over everything, but why hasn't Jesus already returned?

———— ✤ ————

J esus has not yet returned because God is not finished with this world! Someday Christ will come again to conquer evil and establish His perfect rule over all creation—but until then, "This gospel of the kingdom will be preached in the whole world as a testimony to all nations, and then the end will come" (Matthew 24:14).

God wants to give everyone an opportunity to know Christ through repentance and faith in Him. The Bible says, "The Lord is not slow in keeping his promise [that Christ will return]. . . . He is patient with you, not wanting anyone to perish, but everyone to come to repentance" (2 Peter 3:9).

At the same time, we are urged to anticipate Christ's return. The last page of the last book of the Bible says, "Come, Lord Jesus!" (Revelation 22:20 NKJV). While only God knows when this will take place, we are told to be ready. "Our salvation is nearer now than when we first believed. . . . So let us put aside the deeds of darkness and put on the armor of light" (Romans 13:11–12). Now is the time to make sure that your hope and trust are in Him and that you are seeking to live for Him. We brush shoulders with darkened souls every day—so let us shine the light of God's love into the lives of those who may open their hearts to Him.

Does God speak to us from Heaven?

———— ✷ ————

G od speaks to the human heart. I have never heard
the voice of the Lord audibly, but the Lord has
spoken to me many times throughout my life.

So how do we recognize His voice? We must first
belong to Him. The Bible says, "Everyone who is of the
truth hears My voice" (John 18:37 NKJV). God's voice
is not bound by man's schemes or inventions.

God speaks through the Bible, His written Word.
This is why I frequently use the phrase *the Bible says*.
The authors of Scripture made it clear that God was
speaking to them and through them. More than three
thousand times they said, "Thus saith the Lord" or its
equivalent. And because "all Scripture is God-breathed
and is useful for teaching, rebuking, correcting and
training in righteousness" (2 Timothy 3:16), we must
not let anything or anyone take the place of the Bible
to guide our lives.

Second, God also speaks in nature. When He created the Heavens and the earth, He gave us an incredible, complex, beautiful, orderly universe. The Bible declares, "For since the creation of the world God's invisible qualities—his eternal power and divine nature—have been clearly seen, being understood from what has been made, so that men are without excuse" (Romans 1:20).

Third, God speaks through His Son, Jesus Christ, who is revealed for us in the pages of the Bible and is the Word of God incarnate. "In the past God spoke to our forefathers through the prophets at many times and in various ways, but in these last days he has spoken to us by his Son" (Hebrews 1:1–2).

Finally, God speaks to us by the Holy Spirit. This may be the "still small voice" of our conscience that will not let us go until we do what is right—or it may be a loud, clear conviction of what God wants us to do. The Bible says, "The lamp of the LORD searches the spirit of a man; it searches out his inmost being"

(Proverbs 20:27). We must never silence that inner voice. We must check what we think it is saying against the Scriptures to be sure that inner voice is true to God's Word—and then we must obey.

Do the angels have anything to do with our lives right now?

—————— ✳ ——————

Although they are largely unseen, angels are constantly at work on our behalf. The Bible calls them "ministering spirits sent to serve those who will inherit salvation" (Hebrews 1:14).

Scripture documents angelic visitations—times when they did become visible—saying they appeared with glorious radiance, being recognized immediately as angelic beings. At other times, however, they were not recognized as angels because they appeared in human form. The Bible says that "some people have entertained [or welcomed] angels without knowing it" (Hebrews 13:2).

The great comfort in knowing that angels minister to believers in Christ is that God Himself sends them to us. "He will command his angels concerning you to guard you in all your ways" (Psalm 91:11). This is a further manifestation of His constant presence, assuring us that we are never alone if we know Christ. The empire of angels is as vast as God's creation. If you believe the Bible, you will believe in their ministry—and take comfort in it.

Is it wrong to yearn for Heaven and pray for God to take us there, especially when we're overwhelmed by sickness or old age or some other problem?

———— ✳ ————

No, it isn't wrong. In fact, if we never yearn for Heaven, it may mean we've become too satisfied, or too preoccupied with our lives right now!

It's easy to become so overwhelmed with our problems that we focus only on what is happening to us at the moment. But they ought to make us focus instead on Heaven and on the hope we have because of Christ. The Lord is with us through our sufferings, and He awaits us as we emerge on the other side of the tunnel of testing—into the light of His glorious presence to live with Him forever.

Remember: Heaven is our true home, and many times we grow homesick for Heaven—especially in the midst of the sin, sufferings, and sorrows of this life. There is a tug at our souls that is homesickness coupled with anticipation.

I often wonder if God, in His sovereignty, allows our eyesight to cast a dim view of the here and now so that we may focus our spiritual eyes on the ever-after. Paul, who knew what it was to suffer, discovered this truth in his own life: "So we fix our eyes not on what is seen, but on what is unseen. For what is seen is temporary, but what is unseen is eternal" (2 Corinthians 4:18). Don't let the burdens and hardships of this life distract you or discourage you. Keep your eyes firmly fixed on what God has promised at the end of the journey: Heaven itself.

Which is more important, learning how to live in this life or preparing for the next life?

────────── ✿ ──────────

Both are equally important in God's eyes. Which wing of an airplane is more important—the right wing or the left? You know the answer: both are equally important, and if either one is missing, the plane simply can't fly. And the same is true of our faith in Christ.

If we concentrate on only one of these, life will be out of balance—or hang *in* the balance. We won't be living the way God wants us to live, nor will we experience the full measure of His blessing and hope that He has in store for those who love Him. James said, "As the body without the spirit is dead, so faith without deeds is dead" (James 2:26).

God is concerned about our lives right now, and the most important thing about the present life is to settle the afterlife. This life gives us a glorious opportunity to prepare for eternity. Most people are living for today with barely a thought of tomorrow. We are so caught up with the affairs of this life that we give little attention to eternity.

But neither can we ignore our responsibilities on earth. Christians in the world are the only real spiritual light in the midst of great spiritual darkness. God has entrusted us with the privilege of living for Him down here. And, thankfully, He also gives us reason to look forward to the glories of Heaven.

How do we stay on course so
we keep spiritually strong and
aren't diverted from the path to
Heaven that God has for us?

———— ✷ ————

The time to deal with spiritual danger is before it
happens, so be on the alert. You've probably heard
the old adage "forewarned is forearmed." This is also
true spiritually.

Think about how different King David's life would
have been if he had guarded against the temptations of
middle age. Instead his life became a downward spiral of
irresponsibility, adultery, murder, and heartache (2 Samuel
11–12). The Bible says, "Above all else, guard your heart,
for it is the wellspring of life" (Proverbs 4:23).

Strengthen your commitment to Christ—*now*. Don't
wait until the storms of temptation, or sickness, or old

age threaten to blow you off-course; *now* is the time to strengthen your faith. The stronger our relationship is with Christ, the stronger our defense against the devil's temptations. Jesus said, "Pray that you will not fall into temptation" (Luke 22:40).

Learn to commit every situation to God, and trust Him for the outcome. God's love for you never changes, no matter what problems you face or how unsettled life becomes. Nothing takes Him by surprise, and He can be trusted to do what is best. The Bible says, "Trust in the LORD forever" (Isaiah 26:4).

Finally, strengthen the relationships God has already given you. Strengthen your relationship with your spouse, your children, your friends, and your fellow believers. When we're isolated or think we don't need others, we become much more vulnerable to temptation and compromise. Everyone has temptations, but some people entertain them.

Finally, take your eyes off temptation and put them on Christ—and remember how Jesus handled His temptations. With each one, He responded to Satan by quoting the words of Scripture, "It is written." Rely on the Word of God to strengthen you and keep your feet on the straight path.

A Final Word
from Billy Graham

I f you and I could sit together for a few minutes to talk about the subject of Heaven, I would very much want to share the following thought with you.

The Bible has much to say about the brevity of life and the necessity of preparing for eternity. Someday this life will come to an end—but what then? The Bible is clear: ahead of us is eternity, either with God in Heaven or in that place of utter loneliness and despair the Bible calls Hell. But we do not need to fear the future because

God has provided the way for us to be saved and to be with Him throughout all eternity. That way is Jesus Christ, who gave His life for us on the cross, and then conquered sin and death and Hell by His resurrection from the dead.

I am convinced that we will never be prepared to live until we are prepared to die. God has a plan for us right now, and life's greatest joy comes from knowing Him and living for Him every day.

If you have never given your life to Jesus Christ, or if you are unsure of your eternal destiny, I invite you to turn to Him now. By a simple prayer of faith, you can give your life to Him today. Perhaps the following prayer will help you make your commitment:

Oh, God, I know I am a sinner. I am sorry for my sins, and I want to turn from them. I trust Christ alone as my Savior, and I confess Him as my Lord. From this moment on, I want to serve Him and follow Him in the fellowship of His church. In Christ's name, I pray. Amen.

If you sincerely prayed that prayer, God heard you

and you are now part of His family forever. Your sins have been forgiven, and His Spirit now lives within you to help you live a new life. And some day He will welcome you into Heaven—your final home.